PRAISE FOR *TITHING*

Doug LeBlanc's collection of profiles of tithers will open your eyes to how giving can be a practice that shapes rather than an obligation that weighs. Along the way, it also breaks down stereotypes of what kind of person tithes. Rather than teaching or preaching stewardship, this book lets givers from across a wide theological spectrum tell their own stories. Their motivations turn out to be as diverse as their backgrounds, and equally varied are the fruits the discipline bears in their lives. If you have not yet "tested God in this," you may find yourself intrigued enough by their stories to try.

Rev. Beth Maynard
Editor, *Get Up Off Your Knees: Preaching the U2 Catalog*

Which of the following best describes a person who tithes: a conservative evangelical, an Episcopal priest, a progressive activist, a pacifist, a Roman Catholic monsignor, a black church pastor, an Eastern Orthodox author, or a Seventh-day Adventist convert from Judaism? Answer: all of the above, of course! Douglas LeBlanc's book explodes stereotypes and demonstrates that tithing has a way of reordering our priorities so that our focus is not on the issues that perpetually divide us but on giving back to the God who gave everything to us in Jesus. These are inspiring, often surprising stories of God's grace at work in unlikely people, unexpected places, and extraordinary ways. At the same time, they prove that the discipline of tithing isn't just for the super-spiritual: it's something we are *all* called to do.

Fr. Nathan J.A. Humphrey
Editor, *Gathering the Next Generation: Essays on the Formation and Ministry of GenX Priests*

THE ANCIENT PRACTICES SERIES

PHYLLIS TICKLE, GENERAL EDITOR

*Stand at the crossroads and look; ask for the ancient paths,
ask where the good way is, and walk in it,
and you will find rest for your souls.*

—Jeremiah 6:16 NIV

TITHING

Test Me in This

Douglas LeBlanc

THOMAS NELSON
Since 1798

NASHVILLE   DALLAS   MEXICO CITY   RIO DE JANEIRO

In honor of my father

Published in Nashville, Tennessee, by Thomas Nelson. Thomas Nelson is a trademark of Thomas Nelson, Inc.

Thomas Nelson, Inc., titles may be purchased in bulk for educational, business, fund-raising, or sales promotional use. For information, please e-mail SpecialMarkets@ThomasNelson.com.

Library of Congress Cataloging-in-Publication Data

Tithing : test me in this / [compiled by] Douglas LeBlanc.
    p. cm.
 Includes bibliographical references.
 ISBN 978-0-8499-0095-2 (hardcover)
 1. Christian giving. 2. Tithes. 3. United States—Religious life and customs. I. LeBlanc, Douglas.
 BV772.T58 2009
 248'.6--dc22

2009031702

Printed in the United States of America
10 11 12 13 14 WC 9 8 7 6 5 4 3 2 1

CONTENTS

ACKNOWLEDGMENTS

I THANK MY FRIENDS DAVID HANDY, TREVA HOUSER, Michael Noyes, Phoebe Pettingell, Vernon Plack, Tim Ridolfi, and David Virtue for their regular questions and encouraging words about my progress toward a complete manuscript.

The warmth of a dinner conversation with Jon Sweeney helped me form a vision for in-person interviews with the tithing believers I write about in this book.

Steve Levin of the *Pittsburgh Press-Gazette* helped me find Rabbi Yisroel Miller. Lee Penn helped me find John Schwiebert and, like other friends, asked about the book regularly.

Maren Tompkins of All Saints Episcopal Church, Pasadena, and Kathy Norquist of Eternal Perspective Ministries coordinated busy calendars and never lost patience with my requests for help.

My parish priest, Charles Alley of St. Matthew's Episcopal Church, Richmond, offered gentle accountability, empowering prayer, and helpful responses to my draft chapters.

My wife, Monica, blessed my decision to set aside other freelance writing and concentrate on this book for a season. At too many points in our marriage, Monica graciously has allowed my editorial passions to diminish our financial security. She also found important relevant passages for the introduction. I am humbled by her generous love.

FOREWORD

The seven ancient practices of the faith were once called the seven ancient disciplines; but times change, and words change with them. The notion of *discipline* fell out of favor over the years, *practices* seeming more voluntary and therefore less foreboding. By any name, however, the seven come into the life of faith as means of monitoring or directing both the workings of the physical body and the passage of time. Three of the seven—fasting, the sacred meal, and tithing—govern the body, its product and its appetite. The other four—the keeping of the hours, the hallowing of the Sabbath, the observance of the liturgical year, and the making of pilgrimage—govern or give contour to the passage of time.

Of the seven, only two seem to most of us to be awkward or, perhaps, even a bit beyond the pale. That is, fasting and tithing seem somehow more private than do the other five—less subject to conversation and easily more subject to omission, even by the devout. Of that pair, tithing is most assuredly the more difficult to discuss; yet ironically, it and the sacred meal were the first of the seven given us to observe. Like the sacred meal, tithing was established so early in our story that Abram, from whom the first tithe was taken by the Melchizedek, was still Abram and not yet renamed as Abraham. Centuries later,

Christian theology was destined to make much of that fact, St. Paul arguing that Levi and all the priestly line had themselves paid tithes when they were "still in the loins of their father, Abraham."

Regardless of how old or how embroidered its history among us is, however, we Christians tend to bristle or resist or retreat when we are instructed by our clergy or our theologians in the requirement laid upon us to tithe. The instinctive reaction is that the organization, whatever "the organization" is in our particular case, only wants our money, and that any concern for the spiritual benefits of the tithe is purely secondary, if not tertiary. Beyond that, and assuming that some of us do surmount that line of instinctive resistance, there is the nagging sense that tithing is legalistic—far more legalistic, in fact, than are any of the other six. It seems, in our post-Reformation minds, to be part of an old order, something that should have passed on with the coming of New Testament grace.

Tithing is, in sum, then, a truly difficult topic to broach and an almost impossible one to treat sympathetically, much less persuasively. I knew that completely and unequivocally when I approached Doug LeBlanc about writing this volume as part of the Ancient Practices Series. He and I have been colleagues and associates for years; and for all those years, I have admired the clarity of his thought, the steady, unobtrusive consistency of his

Christian devotion, and his quite remarkable skill in making complicated things clear to the rest of us. He seemed to me, therefore, to be the logical choice for writing about this, the most difficult of the ancient seven.

To say that Doug was enthusiastic in his response and filled with eagerness for the project would be about as far from the truth as one could get. It was more a matter of considerable silence, then a question or two, and then the only possible comment, "I'll have to pray about it." He did, and the result is in your hands now as you read this.

In true LeBlanc fashion, he has chosen not to address tithing in long essays about its history among us or with critiques and tedious theological arguments. Instead, in what I think was a stroke of genius or the angels or both, he has chosen to discover men and women who do tithe and are willing to say, publicly and on the record, why they do so. It is their stories in their words that Doug has collected here.

Will this book turn its readers into tithers? Who knows? And perhaps that is not even the point. Perhaps the point is that reading this book will convince us, first, that tithing is possible and, second, that it is one the seven practices for very good and formative reasons. After that, whether we choose to assume the discipline or choose to not assume it is a matter for each of us to decide in prayer. The difference for all of us, though, will be that none of us will ever again be able to occupy a default position of taking no position. In reading, we will have discovered that each of us must decide, just as we will have seen for ourselves what it is we are deciding.

Phyllis Tickle
General Editor
Ancient Practices Series

INTRODUCTION

IN THE EARLY 1990S, I WAS PART OF A HOME BIBLE STUDY connected to a small church in Colorado Springs. It was the first time I had lived in any city other than my birthplace of Baton Rouge, Louisiana. This home group, and others that preceded it, gave me a sense of belonging—not merely in a city and state that were entirely new to me, but also with brothers and sisters in a Christian church. My memories of these home groups are mostly warm ones.

One memory, while not distinctly unpleasant, still leaves me perplexed nearly twenty years later. I remember more than one meeting in which one of our members inveighed against tithing as a mere legalism, a way for modern Christians to escape the much costlier demands of authentic discipleship. This brother was especially keen on arguing that God wants everything we call our own, not merely 10 percent of it.

All of this was fine as theological fodder and as something to meditate on between meetings, but our meetings were taking place in modern suburbia. Members of our group were not known for giving away vast quantities of money, serving in soup kitchens together, or doing much of anything more than meeting together in perfect comfort, drinking coffee or soda, and discussing our faith as something that made our already pleasant lives more pleasant still.

Since then, something in me has felt skeptical when I encounter prosperous American Christians who speak of tithing in tones that sound almost contemptuous, who write joyless books about the very notion of tithing as pastorally insensitive, or who dismiss Christian leaders as opportunists who ought to find honest work in some other form of sales.

I grew up in a home in which tithing was not the norm until I was a teenager. My brother became a Christian through the Jesus Movement. My bewildered father, a gentle soul and World War II veteran, became convinced that my brother had gone off the deep end and began reading the Bible—in search, I think, of a passage in which Jesus urged people to follow him, but not to be excessive about it. Within a year, both my parents came to faith through a renewal movement called Faith Alive.

My father soon announced that our family would transfer from the pious but excessively formal parish in which I grew up to another Episcopal parish, which hosted the Faith Alive weekend that changed our family's life. Also within a year, or at least so it seemed, my father announced that he and Mom would begin tithing. Mom loudly resisted, for a time, but soon enough she realized that Dad was committed, and when the newly converted Lester Louis LeBlanc was committed to something he believed God was calling him to do, resistance was futile.

From that day on, the lesson was lived out before my eyes: my parents tithed off their gross income, and it went to our newfound spiritual home. Dad believed the matter was clear enough in Malachi 3:10: "'Bring the whole tithe into the storehouse, that there may be food in my house. Test me in this,' says the LORD Almighty, 'and see if I will not throw open the floodgates of heaven and pour out so much blessing that you will not have room enough for it.'"

Dad read Scripture faithfully, and he had an almost intuitive sense for cutting to the spiritual heart of a question. I loved to talk about theology with Dad, who had to drop out after elementary school, because what he lacked in education he overcame with wisdom and humility. My theological conversations with Dad never encompassed the Fathers of the church. I was too young to give much thought to the Fathers, and if Dad read them, he did not try to counter my callow opinions by rubbing my face in his deeper learning.

My father died in 1992, after heart surgery that was a technical success but led to a month in intensive care and an attack of pneumonia. I know that Dad would be pleased to recognize, in the Fathers, an affirmation of the principles he lived by when he decided that the LeBlancs would be a tithing household.

The Didache ("The Teaching"), more fully known as *The Teaching of the Lord to the Gentiles by the Twelve Apostles*, stresses the importance of Christians giving generously:

> Give to everyone who asks you, and do not demand it back, for the Father wants something from his own gifts to be given to everyone. Blessed is the one who gives according to the command, for he is innocent. . . . Do not be one who stretches out the hands to receive but withdraws them when it comes to giving. If you earn something by working with your hands, you shall give a ransom for your sins. You shall not hesitate to give, nor shall you grumble when giving, for you will know who is the good paymaster of the reward. . . . But every genuine prophet who wishes to settle among you is worthy of his food. Likewise, every genuine teacher is, like the worker, worthy of his food. Take, therefore, all the first fruits of the produce of the wine press and threshing floor, and of the cattle and sheep, and give these first fruits to the prophets, for they are your high priests. But if you have no prophet, give them to the poor. If you make bread, take the first fruit and give in accordance with the commandment. Similarly, when you open a jar of wine or oil, take the first fruit and give it to the prophets. As for money and clothes and any other possessions, take the first fruit that seems right to you and give in accordance with the commandment.[1]

A passage from *The Conferences* of John Cassian speaks more explicitly of tithing as the starting point of Christian giving:

And so if even those who, faithfully offering tithes of their fruits, are obedient to the more ancient precepts of the Lord, cannot yet climb the heights of the gospel, you can see very clearly how far short of it those fall who do not even do this.[2]

In the Fathers, we see not only an assumption that Christians ought to continue the Jewish custom of tithing, but also some attention to how Christian leaders ought to distribute these gifts:

Let [the bishop] use those tenths and first-fruits, which are given according to the command of God, as a man of God; as also let him dispense in a right manner the free-will offerings which are brought in on account of the poor, to the orphans, the widows, the afflicted, and strangers in distress, as having that God for the examiner of his accounts who has committed the disposition to him. Distribute to all those in want with righteousness, and yourselves use the things which belong to the Lord, but do not abuse them; eating of them, but not eating them all up by yourselves: communicate with those that are in want, and thereby show yourselves unblameable before God.[3]

One of the Christians I write about in these pages, Frederica Mathewes-Green, cited three of the saints of the early church, and in turn she was drawing from research by the work of Randy Alcorn, who had already talked with me about his life in giving:

- "The Jews were constrained to a regular payment of tithes; Christians, who have liberty, assign all their possessions to the Lord, bestowing freely not the lesser portions of their property, since they have the hope of greater things." (Irenaeus)
- "Tithes are required as a matter of debt, and he who has been unwilling to give them has been guilty of robbery. Whoever, therefore, desires to secure a reward for himself . . . let him render tithes, and out of the nine parts let him seek to give alms." (Augustine)
- "If anyone shall not do this he is convicted of defrauding and supplanting God." (Jerome)[4]

I have a lively theological curiosity and have worked as a religion writer for most of my career, but I am no theologian or exegetical writer. To the extent that I am capable of exhortation or teaching, it is mostly through telling the stories of other people's lives. I am prone to a near fundamentalism that is common among old-school journalists:

it's not about you, and keep the first person singular out of your narrative as much as possible. In these pages, I try to limit the first person singular to what background is important to my earlier experiences, in several cases, with the people I am writing about.

In writing these stories, I traveled to seven states and a dozen cities within those states. I make no pretense of this brief book being an exhaustive treatment of tithing or the theology related to it. It is more of a journalist's pilgrimage, one in which my subjects discuss how tithing—or a still larger vision of God's abundant generosity—has affected other aspects of their spiritual lives. Of necessity, some chapters spend more time on the broader spiritual story of these lives than on the details of their tithing.

Tithing tends not to be accompanied by daily or even weekly reflection. Often it is more of a background habit, a reminder that our lives are not our own.

Unlike daily, structured prayer or time spent reading Scripture, tithing tends not to be accompanied by daily or even weekly reflection. Often it is more of a background habit, a reminder that our lives are not our own. Tithing is like prayer in the sense that God is working out his purpose and generously offers us a voluntary place in his purpose. God no more needs the money that flows through our bank accounts than he needs to be informed, through prayer, about the ways in which we hope he will intervene in our lives.

Instead, God is at all times bringing healing and redemption into our world and, to the extent we are ready to cooperate in those goals, God will use us. As we open our otherwise tight grip on what we think of as our money, we begin to realize it has come our way only by the grace of God. As we draw closer to people who need the compassion of Christ, we end up—perhaps even unwittingly—drawing closer to God. It is all God's idea and work, ultimately, but we may choose to become his instruments.

1

CONTINUITY IN THE TRADITION

Gregory and Frederica Mathewes-Green

IN THE SUMMER OF 1991, FREDERICA MATHEWES-GREEN attended the Episcopal Church's 69th General Convention, which met that year in Phoenix. I had admired Frederica's witty articles in the national newsletter of Feminists for Life, which she edited for a few years, and this convention was my first opportunity to meet a woman who was quickly becoming one of my favorite writers. From a distance, I saw Frederica handing out free copies of a document printed on a modern imitation of parchment. The document was the Baltimore Declaration, an effort by six Episcopal priests—including Frederica's husband, Father Gregory—to identify ten points of theological struggle for the church. The closest the declaration came to causing any change in the Episcopal Church was the publication of a thoughtful and largely ignored book,

Reclaiming Faith: Essays on Orthodoxy in the Episcopal Church and the Baltimore Declaration.[1]

I interviewed Frederica during that convention, and I have forgotten most of what we talked about. What I remember, though, is her crying. That year's convention featured a daily morning Bible study combined with the Holy Eucharist. Deputies, bishops, journalists, and visitors gathered together at round tables in a vast and gloomy exhibit hall to read Scripture together and discuss what they thought God might be saying to the convention on any given day.

One morning the text told the wonderful story of John the Baptist leaping for joy, in utero, merely upon hearing the voice of the pregnant Blessed Virgin Mary as she greeted her cousin Elizabeth. Frederica, who was attending convention not only to help promote the Baltimore Declaration but also to volunteer with NOEL (the National Organization of Episcopalians for Life), pointed out the clear pro-life lessons to be drawn from this passage. Frederica's tablemates disagreed with this plain-sense reading of the text. As Frederica told me about this encounter, she cried, explaining that she was not crying because her feelings were hurt but because she was so heartbroken for the church. Frederica and I have been friends ever since.

The General Convention of 1991 was the final national convention that Frederica attended as an Episcopalian.

The convention's anemic response to the Baltimore Declaration, and its refusal to affirm that Episcopal clergy ought to limit their sexual activity to the covenant of marriage, convinced the Mathewes-Greens that they should think about serving in another Christian church. They considered the Roman Catholic Church and what are called continuing Anglican churches—bodies that broke away from the Episcopal Church after it decided to ordain women to the priesthood and adopted a modern version of the Book of Common Prayer (1979). Frederica had attended Virginia Theological Seminary at the same time as her husband, as they both explored whether to become Episcopal priests. When the Mathewes-Greens decided to leave the Episcopal Church, they ultimately joined the Self-Ruled Antiochian Orthodox Christian Archdiocese of North America, a branch of Orthodoxy that has been most pastoral toward Protestants—evangelical Protestants in particular—whose search for a deeper spiritual life has led them toward the East. Frederica told her family's story in her book *Facing East: A Pilgrim's Journey into the Mysteries of Orthodoxy.*[2]

During their childhoods, Gregory was Episcopalian and Frederica was Catholic. They made no pretense of Christian faith when they met each other, and Frederica read a Hindu prayer during their wedding. They were hippies, Frederica was a self-described hairy-legged feminist, and their spirituality was syncretic. On their honeymoon, however, Frederica found herself kneeling before a statue of Jesus and hearing the unmistakable yelps of the Hound of Heaven. When they attended seminary together in 1974 and 1975, they were still zealously renewed Christians— and they began tithing. It was not an easy commitment to make, but it would shape the rest of their life together as Christian disciples.

IMPOVERISHED SEMINARIANS

"We were both new Christians, new to seminary, and, for me, new to the Episcopal Church," Frederica said. "I'm not sure what it was that inspired us to begin tithing. I remember that we were doing it right from the beginning, during our seminary years. We were janitors at Church of the Resurrection; we each got twenty dollars a week, and that was our only income, apart from our being on work-study scholarship. We might have gotten a little bit of income from the work we did at the seminary. So for each twenty dollars, we put two dollars in the basket."

"I'm not sure what it was that inspired us to begin tithing. I remember that we were doing it right from the beginning."

Gregory said, "We knew it was one of those things that committed Christians, biblical Christians, did, and obviously it said something about our commitment of our material things to God."

Frederica recalled their financial struggles during their time in seminary: "Our rent was one hundred dollars a month, and our weekly food budget was ten dollars. I remember it was a splurge to get a container of yogurt. We were vegetarians that year. That helped us save a little bit of money, that first year in seminary. We were extremely poor, poorer than most people would admit. I remember they had just invented ziplock bags, and I was at a school picnic or something, and I was saving the bags and washing them out and putting them out to dry. One of the other students teased me about exaggeratedly acting like I was poor, but I *was* poor. We hadn't bought a box of ziplock bags. My dad had sent us something in several bags, so we saved those bags and kept rewashing them. I didn't buy a mop, because it was eight dollars, and I could mop the floor with a sponge. It was a real sacrifice—to give 10 percent of twenty dollars is a large sacrifice—but we felt very determined about it from the beginning. In thirty-four years of marriage, we have never *not* tithed. Every month we've given 10 percent or more."

"I think we were aware that being truly committed Christians was going to be a life-changing thing, and there wasn't going to be any part of our lives that wasn't touched by that, so it had to mean something for our pocketbooks," Gregory said. "We certainly were biblically literate enough to know what the tithe was."

"I remember a little controversy we were in at the time," Frederica said of her senior year, when she was a part-time student. "We were on campus a couple of days a week, and I didn't want to pay two dollars for the campus lunch. In the cafeteria it was family style; everybody put in two dollars and they put the dishes on the table, but I wanted to bring food from home. The fear was that I hadn't paid and that I might eat some of the food out of the bowls as I sat there eating my sandwich. The administration was very insistent that I put in my two dollars. 'It's just two dollars, that's all you've got to pay.' But I was the one paying the bills, and I knew that we just didn't have an extra two dollars, so I wanted to bring my peanut-butter sandwich. The decision, I guess to force my hand, was that I was not allowed to come into the dining room unless I paid two dollars. So I'd go to classes, talk to my classmates, say good-bye, and then sit in the lobby and eat my sandwich. I think eventually they decided it was safe to let me back in. I think I was allowed to have some of the coffee, but none of the food."

Frederica laughs heartily as she recalls the resolution of this standoff. Gregory describes her as "holding court" while eating in the spacious lobby of the refectory, as her fellow students often gathered around to commiserate with her.

A SECOND POVERTY

Gregory and Frederica speak fondly of this time, as they believe it established patterns of generosity and trust in God that served them well, especially when Gregory made the financially costly decision to leave a well-paying career as an Episcopal priest and to plant Holy Cross, a new Antiochian Orthodox mission in metropolitan Baltimore. Gregory refers to that period as "our second poverty."

Frederica landed a full-time job in 1992 in which she helped work on a pro-life referendum for Maryland. Knowing the financial sacrifices that lay ahead, Gregory and Frederica saved all the income from Frederica's job so they could use it as a cushion in the future. "As we were looking toward becoming Orthodox, we were quite nervous about it, because we had three children, and we'd have to find health insurance somehow, and we'd have to move out of the rectory," Frederica said. "I kept saying, 'Lord, if you give us ten tithers, we will have our church.' We were surprised, as we kind of canvassed the Episcopal parish, that not very many people wanted to join us. We thought that in a high Episcopal church, you just jump off that onto the escalator and go to the slightly higher Orthodox Church. We were surprised that we didn't get very many takers—more arrived as the year went by, but not right away. I kept saying, 'Ten tithers make one income.' I kept praying, 'Give us ten tithers,' and we got five.

"It was very threadbare there for a while. Right from the start, the church decided what Gregory's income was going to be, and it was $1,500 a month or something. It was quite low. They determined that this was our income from February 14, 1993, the first day we had worship, but they couldn't pay it, so month after month went by and we would draw on our savings to pay him the salary, and the church would still owe us. But we kept tabs of how much was owed, and within those first three years it was all paid off. They got to where they could pay a salary and then pay a little bit more to make up the prior shortfall. It's another example of how God brings things together. If it hadn't been for that job with the referendum, I don't know what we would have done. But everything was arriving at the time it was needed, not before, and we were able to make it work."

Gregory wondered during some weeks and months whether he should drive a truck for United Parcel Service. "Looking back, you can see it so much clearer. But as we all know, sometimes being in the midst of creative activity, you don't always know that it's increasingly getting better," he said.

"We insisted that the church tithe to the diocese, and the diocese at that point was providing very little financial support for mission priests," Frederica said. "They sent us $200 a month, and our mission's income was about $2,000 a month, so we sent them $200 a month back. These identical checks would cross in the mail as they supported us and we paid our tithe to the diocese."

For the first several years of its life, Holy Cross met in a community center near Catonsville. In 1997 it bought a church building in Linthicum, near Baltimore-Washington International Airport. The Mathewes-Greens live just around the corner from the church. The building they bought was constructed for a Methodist congregation and had become Full Gospel Mission Church, a Korean congregation, by the time Holy Cross purchased it. The members of Holy Cross poured hundreds of hours into transforming it from a Pentecostal worship space into the icon-rich and incense-friendly church it is today.

As Holy Cross has grown, Gregory has worked his way back toward a reliable income and Frederica has developed a vocation as a prolific author (nine books) and speaker (pro-life groups, churches, college lectures). "As things have gotten better, as Holy Cross Church has put down roots and thrived, I decided (I think it was a year and a half ago) to actually break through the wall to 20 percent," she said. "We gave 20 percent for a year, kind of nervous, but turned out great. It's so true that you can't outgive God."

AN ANCIENT TRADITION

In Eastern Orthodox theology, the Mathewes-Greens have found an anchor for a spiritual discipline they had begun in the mid-1970s, and a deeper explanation for what that spiritual discipline is meant to achieve. "When we became Orthodox, it didn't feel like a radical departure from our sense of what tithing was about and stewardship questions," Gregory said. "It felt like a deepening of it, and we could see much more continuity in the tradition. We could see almost immediately the connection with the whole idea of spiritual disciplines, of the Orthodox emphasis on *theosis*—being like God, growing into the image of God.

"Since clearly one of God's characteristics is generosity—the overflowing of his compassion, his love, and his self-giving—there are different ways the church gifts us in exercising that in ourselves. When we give, the muscle grows, the God-likeness. In the Sermon on the Mount, where Jesus talks about prayer and fasting and almsgiving, those three seem to have a special connection—not just because Jesus talked about them in the same sermon, but also because they're three facets of the Christian life that demonstrate our commitment to the dominion of God over everything and also give us ways to internalize that work.

"By all that, I mean that the dominion of God is over the whole material world. We're given some control over it, but we demonstrate that we know he has the lordship and the dominion, because we tithe. It's even kind of a sacramental illustration, I think."

"The Orthodox continuity with the ancient practices was something we frankly didn't believe until we had been in the church for a while, and we saw that they really fasted on Wednesday and Friday, and maintained other practices from the first century onward. You can just drop into the devotional literature or the records at any point in history, in all of these different ethnic backgrounds, out of touch with each other for centuries, and find that the practices are still the same," Frederica said.

> *"All these practices are training wheels toward*
> *learning how to live fully in the kingdom."*

Gregory cites author Randy Alcorn's image of tithing as a set of training wheels for Christians who want to become serious about their giving. He believes the same is true of fasting. "All these practices are training wheels for learning how to live fully in the kingdom," he said. "At this point in our lives, we need the training wheels, for the most part. Tithing is a really good example, because it may feel like a constriction at first, like training wheels, but after a while grace does move a person to a place where, in a sense, you can take those wheels off and feel truly more generous in your heart, not having to worry so much at the end of the month, 'Did we give the 10 percent?' It's less about the mechanics of it than the growth that really does happen into grace.

"I would say it's really the same dynamic in most of the spiritual disciplines. We come into a fallen world as fallen people, and our relationship to the fallen world is just not as it was meant to be by God. I don't get it right in relation to money; I don't get it right in relation to my stomach; I don't get it right in relation to the use of time or any of these things. In the tradition, there are these great mechanisms and disciplines that help me get it right."

Looking back on their decades of tithing, Gregory and Frederica see consistent evidence of God's faithfulness and his call on them to grow in generosity. "Things have been tougher sometimes, financially, but there's never really been a strong temptation to stop tithing," Gregory said. "What there has been is a realization that we really can give more. God has given us so much, not just financially but in so many different ways, that one of the ways we can clearly give back is by supporting various ministries and outreach and so forth beyond the tithe, which we always give to 'the storehouse,'[3] which we understand as being the church."

"Even at the beginning, we could see that tithing did not make us impoverished," Frederica said. "In fact, somehow we ended up having more money. There were a couple of times, that first year in seminary, we went and looked in the savings account and mysteriously found an extra fifty dollars there that we hadn't put in. That happened at least twice, and we were never able to discover where it came from. (That was in the day when you actually would give them the bank book, and they would stamp it and give it back.) We would get unexpected refunds, bonuses, or things we were never looking for.

"When we tithe, the blessings keep flowing in faster than we can bail them out again."

"That has continued to happen—over and over, things we had expected to pay for would somehow be free, or money that we weren't looking for would just land in the mailbox. It feels like bailing out a leaking boat. When we tithe, the blessings keep flowing in faster than we can bail them out again."

2

SO THAT OTHERS MAY SIMPLY LIVE

Ron and Arbutus Sider

IF YOU'RE TRAVELING ONLY A FEW HUNDRED MILES TO interview the author of *Rich Christians in an Age of Hunger*,[1] somehow it feels more fitting to ride a train than to book a flight. I didn't know the address for Ron and Arbutus Sider's home as I set out on a chilly March morning to talk with them. I rode Amtrak's Silver Meteor from Richmond to the Thirtieth Street station in downtown Philadelphia and then hopped on a commuter train for a brief ride to the Queen Lane station. I called Ron Sider's cell phone number, and within minutes he picked me up in the family car. It's a short drive from the station to the Siders' home, and when I noticed some of the street names in this neighborhood just off Germantown Avenue, my little gray cells came alive. Could it be? Was this the neighborhood of the late and mourned magazine *The Other Side* and its sister ministry, Jubilee Fellowship?

This was the place, and the Siders lived in this same home when the magazine and Jubilee were in their prime. It would be difficult to overstate the importance of *The Other Side* in developing many evangelicals' social consciences from the mid-1960s onward. By the time *The Other Side* closed in late 2004, it had become mostly a voice of liberal Protestantism, although it belonged to the Evangelical Press Association until the end. In its best days, *The Other Side* was the magazine most likely to make evangelicals struggle with the gospel's implications for racial justice, capital punishment, or the relation between sugar and global poverty.

The Siders bought this home in 1975 for $15,000, as part of a multihouse community that at its peak attracted thirty-five adults living in a six-block area. The late John Alexander, son of *The Other Side*'s founding editor and a respected author in his own right, lived across the street. Richard K. Taylor, coauthor with Ron of *Nuclear Holocaust and Christian Hope*,[2] also belonged to Jubilee.

Members of Jubilee shared cars and tools and encouraged one another to live simply. Within small groups, members of the community disclosed their tax returns to each other and discussed how they spent their incomes. Speaking of taxes: the Siders have never had a full audit by the IRS, although the service did challenge the Siders' charitable giving a few years ago. "I didn't even have to supply them with all the cancelled checks," Ron said. "They were satisfied with a copy of the check ledger."

Jubilee thrived for about five years, but the Siders broke from it in 1980. Within about eighteen months, Jubilee disintegrated. "I thought that what we were trying to do was right," Ron said. "If you really work hard at Christian community and share deeply, you inevitably hurt each other. You can't live that close together and not have real fights and disagreements." The hope, the Siders said, was that continued conversation, prayer, and open-ness to change would lead to reconciliation and unity. That unity did not come about. The Siders, among others, withdrew from Jubilee but remained in their home in Germantown. Ron said that the failure of Jubilee was one of the great disappointments of his life.

FROM ONTARIO TO NEW HAVEN

What has drawn me to talk with the Siders is an idea that ultimately grew into the book *Rich Christians*: the proposal of a graduated tithe. The idea is fairly simple: Family members agree to a base amount of what they need to live on for a year. They tithe on that base amount. For every additional $1,000 of income they receive, they increase their giving by 5 percent. In *The Graduated Tithe*—an InterVarsity Press booklet published in 1978, one year after *Rich Christians*—Ron mentioned that his family had agreed to a base amount of $8,000 (for Ron, Arbutus, and their three children).[3]

Talking to the Siders in their comfortable and aging home, I soon realized that the graduated tithe is not the central focus of their financial discipleship as Christians. Instead, the theme that the Siders return to again and again is simple living. It's right there on the opening page of *The Graduated Tithe*: "*The rich must live simply that the poor may simply live.*—Dr. Charles Burke (1975)"[4]

The graduated tithe is not the central focus of their financial discipleship as Christians. Instead, the theme that the Siders return to again and again is simple living.

Both Ron and Arbutus grew up immersed in such teachings—she as the fourth child of a family living in an Amish and Mennonite community, and he as a son of the Brethren in Christ. Both communities stressed simplicity, economic sharing, the need to resist a proud and materialistic culture, not using extravagant display, and striving for peace. They were both born in 1939 and both grew up in Southern Ontario, Canada.

They moved to the United States for Ron to pursue graduate studies at Yale, where he earned both a master's degree and a PhD. He took a leave of absence from his doctoral studies to earn a bachelor of divinity from the Yale Divinity School. While attending the divinity school, Ron did interim ministry at a local church.

One weekend, Ron was preparing a sermon on world hunger. His usual approach to a sermon was to describe a problem, draw lessons from relevant Scripture verses, and suggest actions that believers may take to address the problem. The idea of the graduated tithe came to him as he worked on the sermon. By 1972, he had developed an article on the graduated tithe for *HIS*, a collegiate magazine published by InterVarsity Press.[5] He later proposed a booklet for IVP on the graduated tithe and on world hunger. As he wrote that book in 1975 and early 1976, "it grew like Topsy and became *Rich Christians in an Age of Hunger*."

During the Siders' years in New Haven, they became aware of a clash between simple living and the styles of dress and home furnishings that were common among Ron's classmates and professors. They noticed, for instance, that other people did not have plastic curtains in their homes. Arbutus cut her long hair and bought a coordinated outfit, including a hat and gloves, to wear at church. "We put much more of an emphasis on the outward appearance than we had ever done before," she said. "We were putting pressures on ourselves because we were adapting to a new culture."

The Siders emphasize that the pressures were self-imposed rather than based on anything said to them. Even so, they were uneasy about being shaped by those self-imposed pressures. "I grew up in a home that was very modest and simple," Arbutus said. "The ability to go to high school was a really big thing for me. [Simple living] was always, for me, part of my faith commitment. I was a good little girl who wanted to follow Jesus."

Fitting in was a concern for several years, and the pressures eased in the fall of 1968, when Ron took a job at an inner-city campus of Messiah College. Ron taught at Messiah for ten years, and they lived at Messiah College's Temple University Campus in North Philadelphia for seven of those years. Arbutus recalls an international student telling her, "Stop putting yourself down. I love your home. I feel very much at home here." Arbutus chokes up as she remembers the moment.

"I can remember the point at which I let go of the burden of having to be like everyone else and reclaimed being who I was," she said. "I reclaimed the freedom of simplicity. The freedom to live simply so others can simply live has been a joy to reclaim. That's what makes the graduated tithe not a burden or an oppressive thing but a guide on this freedom journey."

While living in New Haven, the Siders did not lose touch with the social consciences of the churches that formed them. Arbutus, who taught in a one-room schoolhouse in Ontario, found work as a teacher in North Haven's public schools. She used a Laundromat in an African-American neighborhood, and her friends worried about her safety. "I was doing just fine until some of our friends learned I was using *that* Laundromat." She never felt imperiled and kept doing her laundry there.

Ron and Arbutus had an education in black-white relations by getting to know their landlord. He was a custodian at Yale who had to work two full-time jobs—plus his income from renting out two apartments above his home—to provide a good income for his family. "We were in their living room, watching on their television set, during the aftermath of Martin Luther King's death," Arbutus said. They also got to share the experience when their landlord's son made return visits from college and asked why progress on civil rights was so slow.

"By the time we moved to North Philadelphia, I was becoming a full-time mom," she said. "After a year or two, it became clear I wanted to be involved in the neighborhood." She became involved in citywide advocacy for students and their parents, and her advocacy included speaking before the city council and school board. "That felt comfortable. I believed in what I was doing."

Arbutus believes she earned a figurative master's degree in systems thinking through those years of activism: "Ron was writing about systemic evil, and I was seeing it on an urban level." She advocated for public schools, but as she listened to inner-city mothers' hopes for their children, she became convinced that private Christian schools also are important. She helped found Philadelphia Mennonite High School, which opened in 1998. The Siders attend Oxford Circle Mennonite Church, which they appreciate for its economic, racial, and educational diversity.

For twenty years, Arbutus had a private practice as a marriage and family therapist. She stepped away from that practice in 2007. She's drawn to work with people in recovery and with couples, helping them to stay together or to get married. "It's a challenge and a real satisfaction to be walking alongside couples like that." For Arbutus, an important concern is consistently spending real time with people in need. She believes that such commitments of time help Christians realize the world of hurt that surrounds them and give them the chance to embody God's compassionate response to suffering. She considers this a crucial question for a comfortable Christian's discipleship: "This year, with whom am I rubbing shoulders who reminds me that the rest of the world does not have what we have?"

"This year, with whom am I rubbing shoulders who reminds me that the rest of the world does not have what we have?"

MAKING ROOM FOR BRAND-NAME SHOES

In the pages of *Rich Christians* and other books, Ron is a fairly strict critic of consumerism. Among his recommendations for resisting consumerism are "laughing regularly at TV commercials" and "developing family slogans like, 'Who are you kidding?' and 'You can't take it with you!'" During our visit he told a story related to this paragraph in *Rich Christians*:

> For a decade, my own savings bank used a particularly enticing ad: "Put a little love away. Everybody needs a penny for a rainy day. Put a little love away." Responsible saving is good stewardship. But promising that a bank account guarantees love is unbiblical, heretical, and demonic. This ad teaches the big lie of our secular, materialistic society. But the words and music were so seductive that they danced through my head hundreds of times.[6]

The bank that Ron mentioned in this paragraph was the Philadelphia Savings Fund Society (PSFS), which sponsored a math contest that the Siders' oldest son, Ted, won as an elementary-school student. The Siders attended an awards ceremony at the top of the high-rise PSFS Building in Philadelphia's central city. Ron ended up sitting at the same table with an executive who was in charge of the ad campaign. He told her about his critique of the ad. She said it was the most successful campaign PSFS had run. She also agreed that its message was immoral.

The relentless message of *Rich Christians*—that more than a billion people live in grinding poverty and that affluent Christians ought to change their own lives to help relieve that suffering—has led some of Sider's critics to accuse him of being a socialist or an ascetic killjoy. As Ron and Arbutus describe it, they strived to apply the principles of simple living in ways that were not burdensome as their children grew up. "It's one thing to apply it when your kids are one and three and quite another when they're in high school and then on to college," Ron said. When the Siders' two sons mentioned the importance of name-brand shoes among their peers, the parents did occasionally relent and agree to buy such shoes. Ron said that keeping cars until they were no longer reasonably functional, staying in their small modest house in an interracial neighborhood, and buying their clothes mostly at thrift stores were the primary ways they resisted the consumerist tide.

Their commitment to simple living affected their approach to vacations, which they usually linked to Ron's speaking engagements. Three times during the 1980s, the formative years for their two sons and one daughter, the family took cross-country camping trips to reach speaking engagements in the West. Those vacations celebrated the freedom of simplicity without losing any important sense of having fun together, Arbutus said.

More recently, Ron and Arbutus thought carefully before they agreed to join another couple in sharing the use of a modest cabin in northern Maine. Each summer they now spend three to five weeks at the cabin. The cabin relies on gas lighting and gas appliances, and the toilet is outside. The location gives Ron ready access to fishing, a hobby he has long enjoyed. "In some ways it's like being in Ontario, where we grew up," Arbutus said. "We don't live in poverty, and we certainly don't live without the very nice benefits of middle-class life," Ron said.

Ron seems mostly amused by charges of asceticism. He speaks warmly of his long friendship with the Christian apologist John Warwick Montgomery, who worried that Ron was an ascetic and invited him to come along to a meeting of a group dedicated to gourmet dining. Ron told his friend that he would gladly tag along, so long as Montgomery paid for the meal. Ron also recalls talking, during a conference where he gave a speech, with a missionary at Columbia Bible College who felt guilty about enjoying large, fluffy towels when she returned to the United States. "Please don't feel guilty," he remembers saying to her. "I want you to delight in that. The material world is good. It's not that God doesn't want you to have any of these goods of the earth. It's a question of balance."

Ron said, "I've never thought that the reason for living more simply was that somehow living more simply was itself a virtue. Asceticism has never been one of my temptations. We really want people to know about Jesus, so we want the missionary task to flourish, and we think God wants people to have economic justice and not live in poverty. It takes resources to do both of those things."

For that matter, the father of the graduated tithe has held that idea with an open hand over the years, and he sounds untroubled that it has not become a widespread practice among his fellow evangelical Christians. "I very seldom meet people who say they've been applying it," he said. "I've never felt that the graduated tithe is a biblical demand that everyone must follow." He estimates that only five to ten times since the publication of *Rich Christians* in 1977 have people mentioned the importance of the graduated tithe in their lives. In contrast, nearly every time he travels, he meets people who thank him for publishing *Rich Christians* and say the book has affected how they live.

Arbutus said the graduated tithe is not an end in itself but a structure for achieving the higher purposes of simple living and supporting the work of God's kingdom. She compared it to the structure provided by a married couple's pledge of lifelong commitment. Despite their longstanding commitment to the graduated tithe, the Siders warn against treating even basic tithing in a legalistic manner.

The graduated tithe is not an end in itself but a structure for achieving the higher purposes of simple living and supporting the work of God's kingdom.

Tithing is not a biblical demand like sexual fidelity or honesty, Ron said. "It's an Old Testament principle that makes enormous sense, and it's a great starting point. I wouldn't say to a desperately poor single mom, 'You've got to tithe or you're disobeying God.'" Indeed, Arbutus has discouraged impoverished people from tithing when it's clear that their income does not allow paying their bills and tithing. "It's fine for impoverished people to give 2 or 3 or 5 percent," she said.

"We are entirely Christ's," Ron said. "Every part of our being is committed to Christ, which means all of our money is his, all of our resources and property and time are his. We need to be asking, 'How does God want me to use my time and my skills and my money?' For most

American Christians, the tithe as the maximum is just absurd—not because it's a legalistic norm, but that, given what the Bible says, and the needs of the world, and our incredible wealth, we ought to be giving a lot more. I think most American Christians are living in sin by the way they spend their money."

3

MISSIONAL LIVING AFTER KATRINA

Jerry and Stacy Kramer

When I visited Father Jerry Kramer and his wife, Stacy, at the Free Church of the Annunciation, two trailer homes no longer dominated the small parking lot on the west side of the church. This normally would be cause for rejoicing, especially on aesthetic grounds, but these were not normal times. Like most of New Orleans, the neighborhood known as Broadmoor was devastated in late August 2005 when the western edge of Hurricane Katrina lashed the city. Katrina came close to fulfilling decades-long predictions of a hurricane leaving greater metropolitan New Orleans entombed in water. The two trailers in Annunciation's parking lot represented the heart of this small Episcopal congregation's post-Katrina existence—not only its survival but also its freshly renewed ministry in Broadmoor.

Jerry negotiated with a dealer in Texas to buy the trailers because he knew the church could not afford to wait for help from the Federal Emergency Management Agency. One trailer served as the church's worship space and emergency housing for a flooded-out parishioner. Another trailer provided office space for Jerry and for the Broadmoor Improvement Association. The association was the rallying point for Broadmoor residents as they fought the city's initial redevelopment plans, which would have rezoned this mixed-income neighborhood—from the poor to the middle class to Walter Isaacson's childhood home—out of existence. From both of the trailers, Jerry and other leaders of Annunciation oversaw the parish's ministry of distributing cleaning supplies, food, clothes, and truckloads of other donated items from across the nation. Because of the trailers' role in the resurrection of Annunciation, the parking lot seemed almost diminished without them.

Walking around the block that houses Annunciation, I missed the trailers less. At Jena Street and South Claiborne Avenue stands the church's restored nave. Creating a small new narthex on the west side has decreased noise from the four-lane, hectic Claiborne Avenue. Before Katrina, an entrance at the back of the church offered no buffer between the street and the worship space. The narthex also gives new prominence to a stained-glass window that depicts Jesus standing on the

Sea of Galilee and reaching for a panicked Saint Peter, after the impulsive Peter tried to join Jesus in walking on water. Before Katrina, that window was above the back door and difficult to notice. Now the window is hard to miss as you walk in from the new side entrance, or if you're walking by on Claiborne after dark. In the months after Hurricane Katrina, Annunciation's nave was so damaged by putrid floodwaters that Jerry urged his people not to expect that they would worship within it again. Bishop Charles Jenkins of the Episcopal Diocese of Louisiana presided over a tearful deconsecration of the nave, which stood on this corner for nearly a century.

Next door to the nave, in the former rectory, Jerry hopes to fulfill a post-Katrina vision for a neighborhood coffeehouse with free Wi-Fi. On the corner of Jena and South Derbigny streets is a neighborhood playground built by volunteers and filled with brightly colored equipment donated by a nonprofit organization called KaBOOM. On Derbigny Street is a former two-story home that's been remodeled to house the church's youth ministry. Between the Youth House and the playground is Gabriel House, another remodeled two-story residence that is now home to the Broadmoor Improvement Association and Annunciation's church offices. Here, in a sunlit office decorated with icons and burning candles, Jerry and Stacy Kramer sat to discuss their life as a tithing couple.

MAKING A COVENANT

Jerry is a perpetual-motion entrepreneur, but Stacy is the reason the Kramers began tithing. When Stacy was twenty-seven, her mother encouraged her to read a book about tithing. The book was by a member of the Unity School of Christianity, and although Stacy does not believe Unity's underlying theology, she found the author's case on tithing both convincing and well grounded in Scripture. Stacy was so persuaded that she wrote an individual covenant with God, modeled after the covenant between Jacob and God as described in Genesis 28:20–22:

> Then Jacob made a vow, saying, "If God will be with me and will watch over me on this journey I am taking and will give me food to eat and clothes to wear so that I return safely to my father's house, then the LORD will be my God and this stone that I have set up as a pillar will be God's house, and of all that you give me I will give you a tenth."

Stacy also was struck by God's call to tithing in Malachi 3:6–12: "It's the only place in Scripture where God says, 'Test me in this,'" Stacy said, contrasting the passage with the repeated warning throughout Scripture against putting the Lord to the test.

In her covenant, Stacy pledged to tithe off her net income for six months. As Stacy honored her promise, her income increased unexpectedly. She worked at a hospital that was imposing a salary freeze, but she received a $7,000 salary adjustment. "To a tither and to God, there is no such thing as a fixed income or a salary freeze," she said. In contrast, she said her life suddenly turned hellish after she decided to skip tithing when money seemed tighter. She worried about money more, and a bill for emergency surgery amounted to roughly the same amount she would have tithed. From this experience, she concluded that God puts his followers' money to use one way or another: "Don't you want to cooperate and experience God's blessings?"

"If you call yourself a Christian, the starting point is the tithe. . . . God likes for you to give sacrificially, to give and not know how you're going to eat."

Stacy grew up poor, and she said that made her focus on material comfort as a young adult. "I'm a born-again cheapskate. I was a taker and not a giver," she said. For Stacy, tithing was the beginning of learning how to give. "If you call yourself a Christian, the *starting point* is the tithe," she said. "God likes for you to give sacrificially, to give and not know how you're going to eat."

TITHING FOR LOVE

Stacy became such an ardent proponent of tithing that she did not want to marry any man who failed to appreciate the importance of the discipline. Tithing was a new concept to Jerry when he met Stacy. Jerry was a stewardship consultant to Catholic dioceses, mostly in Texas, and thought he was doing well to give twenty dollars during the weekly offering. Jerry said that most of the parishioners he worked with as a stewardship consultant were giving one-half of 1 percent of their income.

Jerry remembers with amusement that his life goal was to be a partner in a Catholic stewardship-consulting firm. He attributes this very precise goal, and his aptitude for the work, to his childhood. Young Jerry had to ask for his allowance each week, making the case for why he deserved it and explaining how he intended to spend it. By his early thirties, Jerry had achieved his life goal. Being a stewardship consultant was lucrative enough for Jerry to earn a six-figure income and for the Kramers, who were married in 1996, to enjoy an upper-middle-class life in a gated community in Houston. They both laugh about their perception during those years that they were struggling to make ends meet. "Your money is where your faith hits the road," Jerry said. "Look at your check register, and you'll know what you're worshipping.

For many years we were worshipping Blockbuster Video and Domino's Pizza."

"Your money is where your faith hits the road. . . . Look at your check register, and you'll know what you're worshipping."

A crucial shift occurred when Jerry decided to become an Episcopal priest. Becoming close with two priests at St. Christopher's Episcopal Church in League City, Texas—Walter Ellis and later Jim Smalley—deepened his sense of calling. Jerry sensed that God wanted more of him than just raising money. "Giving is essentially a fruit of faith and not the end in itself," Jerry said. "I knew the bigger issue was calling and challenging people to deeper faith. It wasn't a crisis of stewardship; it was a crisis of discipleship. If you disciple people effectively and lead them to real, transformative faith, the money takes care of itself."

Jerry had explored a possible call to the priesthood much earlier in life while he was still a Catholic. Now Jerry felt further called to serve as a missionary in Africa. His seminary experience had prepared him for missionary service, and Africa now seemed to beckon. Jerry wanted to experience the flourishing church there and participate in what God was doing in East Africa. First, though, the Kramers had a financial hurdle they wanted to clear. Even with Jerry's six-figure income, the Kramers had accumulated $30,000 in credit-card debt.

In the early years of their marriage the Kramers tithed on their net income, and Jerry thought that tithing meant giving 5 percent to your church and 5 percent to a charity. Stacy pressed for giving the first 10 percent to the church where they worshipped—she calls it giving "10 percent to your house." The Kramers resolved together that they would begin tithing on their gross and asked God to guide them in clearing their credit-card debt. Both God and the Kramers honored their ends of that covenant, and the Kramers have tithed off their gross income ever since.

KATRINA CHANGES EVERYTHING

After several years of back-and-forth travel, the Kramers and their three children served as missionaries in Tanzania for fourteen months before returning to the United States. In late January 2005, Jerry interviewed with Annunciation's search committee. Within a week, the committee invited him to become the church's next rector.[7] Only a few months into Jerry's time as rector of Annunciation, Hurricane Katrina slammed into the Gulf coasts of Louisiana and Mississippi. Six feet of water flooded the church and its parish hall for about three weeks. Gangsters broke into the parish hall and made the upstairs room their hangout. Jerry said that nurses at Baptist Memorial Medical Center, located across Claiborne from the church, told him they saw the gangsters come and go by boat, trading drugs and exchanging gunfire by day, eating and drinking in the parish hall by night.

The Kramers had evacuated safely to Baton Rouge when Katrina approached the coast. A week after Katrina struck, Jerry returned to survey the damage at Annunciation. After stumbling along Napoleon Avenue and finally borrowing a fishing boat from neighboring merchants, a bewildered Jerry found his way to the church. Upstairs in the parish hall, he found junk food, switchblades, and a battery-powered boom box still playing music—all left behind by the looters who had riffled through the building in search of any valuables they could steal.

In the nave, Jerry found the sort of catastrophe caused by floodwaters. Pews had moved throughout the room and were still floating in the hazardous water, which had become, across greater New Orleans, a toxic and revolting mix of fuel, garbage, feces, and decaying bodies. Jerry said that as he stood in the nave, both looking upon the damage and being filmed for a televised news report, he could not imagine where to begin putting the pieces back together.

Annunciation began putting the pieces back together

by trying to help relieve the suffering of its neighbors. It not only distributed relief supplies from its parking lot, but with the help of St. Luke's Episcopal Church in Baton Rouge, it offered similar help several miles east to the Lower Ninth Ward, where devastation was even worse than in Broadmoor. Jerry recruited Robert Perry, a bus driver for the city of New Orleans and a member of Annunciation, to drive an RV on weekdays and help distribute the supplies from the parking lot of an abandoned Walgreens. Robert had evacuated to Atlanta and was planning a return to Delaware, where he grew up, but this new mission convinced Robert to return to New Orleans and to stay.

Annunciation helped launch a new Episcopal mission in the Lower Ninth Ward, which met in one of the few scattered homes there that was not totally destroyed by Katrina. The Diocese of Louisiana asked the Walgreen Company if it would donate the abandoned store for continuing relief and development work in the Lower Ninth Ward. The company agreed, and All Souls Church found a larger space in which to worship. When the archbishop of Canterbury met with the Episcopal Church's bishops in New Orleans in late September 2007, he visited the building and blessed the congregation with holy water. Neighborhood children watched as Rowan Williams, the archbishop of Canterbury, with his shock of wiry hair and a full beard, blessed the church amid billowing incense.

BECOMING A MISSIONAL CHURCH

Two and a half years after Hurricane Katrina struck, as I listened to Jerry and Stacy Kramer describe how the storm transformed their struggling little parish, I cautiously asked whether they felt the church was somehow stronger—better, even—because of going through the ordeal together. Jerry sensed my hesitation. "There's no need to dance around the issue," he said. "Stacy and I have discussed this many times, and the answer is yes. Even today, knowing all that it would entail, we would choose to go through it again. Our marriage was pushed to the brink, but we have a tighter bond than ever because of what we went through together."

"God is always up to something good. Our purpose as a church is to find out what God wants to do through us and be available to him."

As Jerry sees it, Hurricane Katrina helped Annunciation move from being a mostly unnoticed neighborhood church, struggling just to survive, to a missional church that the residents of Broadmoor now know with affection because of its role in preserving the neighborhood and helping people in their moments of greatest need. "God is a missional God," Jerry said. "God is always up to something good. Our purpose as a church is to find out what God wants to do through us and be available to him."

Katrina sharpened Annunciation's focus because it clarified which members were ready to be missional. In the wreckage after Katrina, Jerry told his congregation that Annunciation "would not be a mere chaplaincy, worshipping a stained-glass window and a prayer book." To those members who wanted to return to what Annunciation was before Katrina, Jerry suggested that several Episcopal parishes along the posh and elegant St. Charles Avenue might be more appropriate places to worship. "I know that many of the old guard didn't sign up for this kind of church. But we had to become something different in the wake of Katrina. A sleepy, inward-looking chaplaincy wasn't going to cut it. I have no problem with people going elsewhere if our church isn't their cup of tea. We know our mandate, and we're unapologetic about it. Go where you're going to be fed. We now seem to feed people who want to make a real difference for our community and for the world."

In the weeks after Katrina, a neighbor who was contemplating suicide stopped by Annunciation's relief center instead. That day, a member of Annunciation listened sympathetically, hugged her, and gave her a Bible. The neighbor became a steady volunteer and a member of Annunciation. Robin Yeager, a kitchen worker at Annunciation, prayed with a parishoner for the first time in her years of working there, and she became a Christian. Before then, Jerry said, she was just treated as hired help.

The parish hall, which had been thoroughly flooded and trashed after Katrina, is now restored. It served as the relief supply warehouse for nearly two years. Rooms on the second floor have been transformed into dormitory-style bedrooms that house volunteers for the long term. Barring another hurricane strike, rebuilding New Orleans could take another decade.

Jerry said that Annunciation has been the site of remarkable cooperation between conservative and liberal Episcopalians. Indeed, Annunciation has hosted volunteer teams from liberal parishes, such as St. Columba's in Washington, D.C., and from conservative ex-Episcopal churches, such as Truro in Fairfax, Virginia, sometimes with overlapping time together. For suburban conservatives, Jerry said, Annunciation provides a chance to encounter the urban poor as more than an abstraction. For wealthy liberal parishes, Annunciation provides hands-on work rather than just a place to send a check. For parishes across the spectrum, New Orleans is a good practice ground for the culture shock of serving somewhere in the developing world. "We're just dangerous and Third World enough to provide that kind of training," Jerry said.

The Kramers do not credit tithing for everything in their spiritual pilgrimage from a gated community in Houston to missionary work in Tanzania and building a missional church in post-Katrina New Orleans. They do say, however, that tithing was an important part of learning to keep material things in perspective, setting aside idols, and trusting entirely in God.

Members of Annunciation gained a deeper appreciation of the generosity inspired by tithing. Despite losing so much and living so precariously, the parish has increased its local giving 60 percent. One day a new member grew cautious about giving away too many emergency supplies and wanted to cut back. A member with more experience stressed Annunciation's teachings about giving freely and trusting God to provide. The next day another truckload of much-needed supplies arrived.

"The focus of biblical tithing is on what you can do, out of a grateful heart, to serve God, not on what you can get out of God."

The Kramers faced a test of their commitment in Christmas 2005, when they were down to a household balance of fifteen dollars and no money to buy gifts for their children. They had already pledged several thousand in support to an orphanage in Tanzania, and they honored the pledge. Then Stacy received a check from a friend in Texas who insisted that she use it exclusively for buying the children's Christmas gifts.

"The focus of biblical tithing is on what you can do, out of a grateful heart, to serve God, not on what you can get out of God," Stacy said. "I don't want a Mercedes-Benz. If someone gave me one, I would give it to another person. I think that as Christians, we are called to be downwardly mobile."

4

EARNEST MONEY

John Schwiebert

PRESIDENT GEORGE H. BUSH IS CREDITED WITH CALLING
Portland, Oregon, "Little Beirut" because of violent pro-
tests that broke out there as he visited the city in 1990.
Metanoia Peace Community United Methodist Church
is resolutely nonviolent, but the posters dotting its slop-
ing yard make clear that this spacious corner of Northeast
Eighteenth and Tillamook streets is not Bush County.
Elsewhere in the yard stands a peace pole, a gift from a
Portland city commissioner, which expresses the wish MAY
PEACE PREVAIL ON EARTH. "Ten Reasons Why the U.S.
Must Leave Iraq" appear at the front door of the building
Metanoia calls the Eighteenth Avenue Peace House.

The Rev. John Schwiebert met me at the door of Peace
House, and we settled into a quiet room to discuss Metanoia
Peace Church's history and its commitment to tithing. John

is a tall and slender man who speaks quietly and deliberately, offers steady and friendly eye contact, and laughs when remembering some of the stranger moments of being a peace activist. Once, when spending the weekend in jail, he and other protesters learned of their impending release as they watched a televised news broadcast. This was news not only to the protesters but also to the jail's guards.

John grew up in Caldwell, Idaho, attended the College of Idaho, and then spent three years at Drew Theological Seminary in New Jersey. He settled in Oregon in 1972. "I've lived more than half my life right here in Portland," he said. John is countercultural but pragmatic—a few times he expressed astonishment at how so many people do not understand the basics of handling money. He's idealistic but candid about times when the community's ideals have not worked out very well. Metanoia, which welcomes people "regardless of age, race, nationality, gender, sexual orientation, economic status, or experience with Christianity or a faith community," hired Joyce McManus, a lesbian, as copastor in 1993. Within two years, 80 percent of the church decided it could not afford to keep her on staff. Metanoia lost some of its members as a result and ultimately paid $60,000 to buy out the interests of McManus and her partner in a nearby home the church had purchased.

Metanoia is a small, intentional community that began forming in mid-1985. In the New Testament, the Greek word *metanoia* refers to changing one's mind, or repenting. The core founders of Metanoia—John and his wife, Pat, and Bruce and Ann Huntwork—knew each other through their longtime involvement in peace protests and nonviolent direct action. Metanoia defines the latter as "active confrontation of specific instances of violence and injustice, sometimes using illegal means (civil disobedience), but only in a manner which is faithful to the principles of nonviolence in word and deed, as practiced by Jesus, Gandhi, the Berrigan brothers and others."[1] Indeed, John recalls that part of his courtship with Pat involved their attending rallies against the Vietnam War.

"We had a sense that the call to Christian discipleship was much more radical than most churches conceived of it."

Metanoia felt like a natural name for the community because of the founders' shared experiences. "Because we were doing nonviolent, Gandhi-style civil disobedience, we were organized into affinity groups. There was a group of us who were Christian, and self-consciously so, and we were part of this other movement that had all kinds of people in it. We needed a name for our affinity group, so we called it Metanoia. That was before we created Metanoia Peace Community. When we later began meeting and talking about a new congregation, Metanoia was a name we were already using," John said. "We had been a part of churches before, and we had a sense that the call to Christian discipleship was much more radical than most churches conceived of it. We talked about things like turning away from rugged individualism, which was rampant in our society, to actually embracing community—not separating ourselves from, but marching to a different drum than the dominant culture. There was certainly a countercultural aspect of it, and we understood Metanoia to imply that. You change direction."

Unlike some other intentional Christian communities in the United States, such as Jesus People USA in Chicago, or The Word of God in Ann Arbor, Metanoia never grew into a membership of several hundred. A history on Metanoia's Web site (www.metanoia.org) tells of thirty adults enrolling in a School of Christian Living "designed to build community and prepare individuals for membership and leadership."[2] Nineteen people completed the course and became Metanoia charter members.

Membership at Metanoia is not simply a matter of placing your name in the church records and showing up for worship at your leisure. A covenant commits full members of the church to these disciplines:

- Participate weekly in the Sunday gatherings of the community.

- Regard all of our personal income and possessions as a resource to be shared, beginning with the tithe (10%).
- Meet regularly with other members in a small Covenant Member Group, where we allow others to hold us accountable for living out this covenant.
- Meet monthly with other members in a gathering of the full membership.
- Devote time daily to meditation, prayer, silence and other acts of devotion, both alone and with others (the journey inward).
- Be in mission to the world, as evidenced in specific acts of compassion and justice (the journey outward).
- Live our lives in response to God's call, seeking guidance from other members in an ongoing process of discernment of that call.
- Support and uphold one another, as together we participate in building up the body of Christ.
- Continue in membership until, in conversation with our fellow members, we have together come to discernment that we are being called to some other place or relationship.[3]

Today, John said, there are sixteen committed members of Metanoia, half of whom live together at Peace House. There are another thirty-five "sojourning members," people who identify with Metanoia's mission but have not signed on to the membership covenant. Worship services at Metanoia normally attract about twenty-five people. Only John and one sojourning member of Metanoia, a civil-rights activist named Lisa Clay, chose to discuss their experiences with tithing.

If a member of Metanoia lives at Peace House, it could seem that asking for a tithe is a bit redundant, like expecting cloistered nuns to wear a veil during their waking hours. Instead, though, the tithe is the starting place for all covenant-committed members of Metanoia to begin a journey into the generosity of God.

"If you become a member of Metanoia, you agree that tithing is the platform in which you enter into membership. You start there," John said. "One metaphor that I like to use, and we talked about it a lot in the early part of Metanoia, was the tithe as earnest money. As with most real-estate transactions, and certainly this house, the process starts with your saying, 'I want to buy this house, and as an indication of my seriousness about this, I'm putting down $10,000 of earnest money, which tells you that I intend to follow through on it.' If the seller follows through and I don't, then the seller gets to keep the money.

"If you become a member of Metanoia, you agree that tithing is the platform in which you enter into membership. You start there."

"We said, okay, what we're aiming for in our community life is to share all things in common, so that nothing you ever receive in any kind of income is a resource that you're not willing to share," he said. "Some of the money you have to keep for yourself, in order to keep yourself from falling into poverty. Some of the money you need to give away to other people. But the tithe, the 10 percent, is your earnest money that you give every month or every week, which is your way of saying I am fully committed to this. 'Seek first the kin-dom of God[4] and all these other things will be added unto you' has been a powerful conviction for us, I think. The more we saw ourselves investing in the kin-dom of God, the less we had to worry about where resources were going to come from. They just seemed to come. That's been powerfully true for us."

CREATING A COMMUNITY

Two things have helped Metanoia's finances: the clean purchase of Peace House, and Pat Schwiebert's career in helping grief-stricken families who lose unborn children or newborns to an early death (www.griefwatch.com).

Pat learned many skills working with dying patients, John said. "At the same time, she had also been doing child-birth education, and when she encountered people whose children died before, during, or after childbirth, she was a real help to them. They told their stories about how sometimes insensitive the hospital staff was, not knowing what to do. Of course staff members felt bad, but they tended to isolate emotionally from the parents. She started teaching and writing about how medical professionals can understand grief and help people. She wrote a book called *When Hello Means Goodbye*,[5] which was addressed to parents, and told them how to help get what they need when they confront that kind of situation, how to deal with their own grief, and how to help others help them with their grief.

"She was working for the Oregon Health & Science University at the time, and Oregon Health & Science University published the book. The foundation was a nonprofit organization, and at a certain point they said, 'We've got too many of these small enterprises, and we ought to spin some of them off.' What we realized was that we were a nonprofit. By that time, we had formed Metanoia Peace Community United Methodist Church. There wasn't enough space up at the Oregon Health & Science University anyway, because the program was growing, so we moved it in here. So now it's a part of Metanoia Peace Community. Since we ship books and other supplies from here, and even do some of the printing here in the basement area, the proceeds from the sale of those materials helps pay the bills. It helps pay property tax and helps pay the costs of maintaining the building. Of course we live here, too, and don't have to pay rent or house payment somewhere else. The amount of money we're able to leverage because of those economies is substantial. We're able to contribute to other groups and to do a significant amount of ministry for our size."

Metanoia purchased Peace House after the Schwieberts saw, during a morning jog, that the building was available. A bank in St. Louis had seized it in a foreclosure. "The price for it was $120,000 in 1986. We didn't have cash. We had a house, and Bruce and Anne had another house. We had already been talking to them about forming this new community and about forming a new church. They said, 'We're in on it if you want to do it.' We knew we would have to come up with the cash, because there was another buyer standing in line who had cash. We went to twenty-six different friends and borrowed money on simple promissory notes, unsecured loans, and we did it in, like, two and a half weeks. We put it all together, handed them the cash, took the title to the house, and then as soon as we got Metanoia formed and incorporated, we deeded the house over to the church.

"We knew there couldn't be any appearance of laundering money or pretending that it belonged to the church when it really belonged to us," John said. "Part of creating the community was that we had essentially renounced private property, and the rest of our lives we expect to live in community with other people and not go out of this life owning anything. It just became a part of our conviction.

"The title has in it that if Metanoia Peace Community should ever cease to exist, the ownership of the property would automatically transfer to the [Portland-based] Oregon-Idaho Conference of the United Methodist Church. I don't know what they'll do with it, but it's very clear that we reserve no rights to it. On the other hand, we had a document written out between the residents of the house and Metanoia Peace Community United Methodist Church Incorporated that said we could live in the house if we paid all the costs for operating it. We do that. Part of the cost comes out of the Grief Watch program. Since I've retired, and the church doesn't have to pay any salary, the church budget agrees to pay half of the utilities."

RESCUED BY A TITHE

Lisa Clay has been a sojourning member of Metanoia since the early 1990s. Lisa said she learned about the importance of tithing from attending small and struggling but Spirit-filled churches in her earlier years. She tells two dramatic stories of her experiences with tithing during her years with Metanoia.

One story involves fellow members of Metanoia coming to her sudden rescue. "One day I was walking down the street and I needed $400. Some terrible thing had happened and I was on a very, very low income, and raising my children pretty much by myself," she said. "I needed $400, and it was really urgent, and I was so down. I heard this horn, and I looked up and there was this family. They were probably having as bad a struggle as I was. She and her kids had gotten some kind of blessing. She and all of her kids gave me their tithes, and it came to $400. It created love, through tithing, just letting the Holy Spirit lead. The exact amount! That kind of thing sticks in your head."

Lisa's other story involves a dilemma she faced after receiving an $80,000 settlement from a civil-rights lawsuit against a store. She hesitated about tithing and was ill at ease until she decided that tithing needed to be her top priority. "I was swimming around, so confused. In my heart I knew something was wrong, and that's what was wrong: I hadn't put God first," she said. "The next day, everything fell into place. It was almost instantaneous." She gave the tithe to Metanoia, which placed the entire $8,000 into the pastor's discretionary fund. John Schwiebert assured Lisa that if more needy families came to her attention, he stood ready to help them through the tithe she had surrendered to God.

5

TREASURES IN HEAVEN

Randy Alcorn

RANDY ALCORN'S COMMITMENT TO THE PRO-LIFE CAUSE cost him his thirteen-year vocation as pastor of Good Shepherd Community Church, located about five miles southeast of his home in the Portland suburb of Gresham. In God's economy, however, Randy developed a much wider pastorate through his popular books, including novels and nonfiction. His books have created a few million dollars in royalties and he has given away all of the royalties to Christian ministries. A few themes thread their way through most of Randy's books: Jesus has redeemed us by his death on the cross, heaven and hell are real, and God calls his people to lives of sacrifice for the sake of his eternal kingdom.

Randy welcomed me to his office behind his home. The office was lined with framed book covers and sports memorabilia. It's definitely guy space, but much tidier than a bachelor's apartment. Randy mentioned that he would need to check his blood sugar periodically. He was diagnosed as an insulin-dependent diabetic in 1985. We both set up recording devices, chose soft drinks from a small refrigerator, and sat to talk about how God is using the son of a tough-minded tavern owner to spread some lessons about the costs of discipleship.

Randy grew up in Portland in a non-Christian household. He began attending Powell Valley Community Church to be around a young woman named Nanci. He became a Christian through that church, and Nanci eventually became his wife. Randy said he was drawn early in his Christian life toward people who made heroic sacrifices for their faith—people like the late Richard Wurmbrand, who was tortured by communists in Romania and later led a ministry called Voice of the Martyrs; and Brother Andrew, who repeatedly risked arrest by smuggling Bibles behind the Iron Curtain. "For several years I didn't give much to the church. Instead I gave a whole lot to parachurch Christian ministries, especially those working with persecuted Christians," he said.

Randy became aware of tithing when his pastor preached on the importance of supporting the local congregation. He remembers that the sermon drew on

Galatians 6:6: "Anyone who receives instruction in the word must share all good things with his instructor."

Randy said he was already giving "significantly beyond 10 percent" outside the congregation. "However, what I determined to do at that point was to give 10 percent to the church. When I gave 10 percent to the church, I sensed the vested interest that I then had. By that time I understood what Jesus was saying in Matthew 6:20–21, in terms of storing up for ourselves treasures in heaven, and when you give to something, where your treasure is, there will your heart be also."

Randy said he was persuaded that tithing was the least he could do for his congregation, and that he never looked on it legalistically. "I was prone even back then to do my homework and research. It just became clear that, as a New Testament follower of Christ, in the most affluent society in human history, there's no way I could ever justify giving less than 10 percent when God had required that, really, of the poorest Israelite. Here I know the grace of Jesus. Why would I not give more? It seemed like a good starting place. I wouldn't have articulated it that way, but looking back, I think that really was what I was experiencing."

"As a New Testament follower of Christ, in the most affluent society in human history, there's no way I could ever justify giving less than 10 percent when God had required that, really, of the poorest Israelite."

Randy earned a bachelor's degree in theology from Multnomah Bible College and a master's degree from Western Seminary, both in Portland. While studying at Multnomah, he became a part-time youth pastor at Powell Valley Community Church. Shortly after completing his master's degree in 1977, he became one of two original pastors at Good Shepherd Community Church, where he remained as a pastor until 1990. He had neither grown bored with his responsibilities nor fallen into moral failure. Instead, he joined a group trying to protect the lives of the unborn at Lovejoy Surgicenter—so named because it is on the corner of Northwest Twenty-fifth Avenue and Northwest Lovejoy Street in Portland. The *Los Angeles Times* reported in 1998 that the facility "performs nearly half of all abortions in Oregon, as well as offering podiatry, vasectomies, tubal ligations and plastic surgery."[1]

GAINING STRENGTH THROUGH BROKENNESS

Randy was among the Christians who participated in pro-life rescues beginning in the 1980s. In fact, one of his books—*Is Rescuing Right?*—made the case for nonviolent civil disobedience at abortion clinics.[2] For Randy and thirty-three other protesters, it proved a costly decision. Allene Klass, owner of Lovejoy Surgicenter, took the protesters to court on charges of trespass and nuisance. She won the case, and the jury imposed a judgment of $8.2 million on the protesters.

Randy already was a published author by then, but royalties were not his primary income when the judgment came down. "Once we gave the books and the royalties completely over to the Lord, book sales dramatically increased, which I think itself was interesting, kind of God's way of saying, 'Put them in my hands, and the causes go to things I'm concerned about, that I have a vested interest in.' I knew I needed to provide for my family. My wife didn't work outside the home, and we didn't want her to. There was any number of things I could do, but the problem was, I couldn't make over minimum wage. Whatever job I was going to do, 25 percent of what was above minimum wage could be garnished. I did not want a dime to go to an abortion clinic. I could work hard, but at the end of the day, if a large chunk of this money was going to an abortion clinic, that was just unthinkable."

Randy resigned as pastor of Good Shepherd, and he founded External Perspective Ministries. "The ministry pays me minimum wage plus benefits so that I can write books, which—by God's grace—are earning millions of dollars," Randy said. "It's crazy, humanly speaking, but it works great."

Randy was not alone in his response: the *Times* also

reported that Lovejoy Surgicenter had collected only about $250,000 of the $8.2 million judgment. The judgment stood for ten years and then was renewed for another ten years. Randy expects the judgment will expire on its twentieth anniversary, but he is not likely to change his financial choices. When the first ten-year judgment period was about to expire, the board of Eternal Perspective Ministries—having no idea that the judgment would be extended—offered to give the Alcorns access to the book royalties. After discussing the offer and praying about it, the Alcorns declined—and soon learned that the judgment had been extended.

Being part of that $8.2 million judgment and being diagnosed as a diabetic have been two of the most powerful experiences in Randy's spiritual life. They have "ultimately been a cause of not only growth but also rejoicing about that growth," Randy said. "My point, of course, is not that those were easy or that they remain easy. They haven't been, and they aren't. But I see such great ways that God has used those things in my life. I was very independent. My health had been good. My father owned a number of taverns and was the most independent human being you have ever known, and he was extremely healthy and strong. Even though I came to Christ when I was in high school, in pastoral ministry I discovered—and the people who worked with me, I'm sure, discovered—that I was self-reliant. Now, I was a Jesus-loving Christian who was seeking to draw upon God's empowerment in what I did. But pretty much I got up, got out of bed, worked long hours, did what I did, and didn't really need to rely on anyone that much.

"When I became an insulin-dependent diabetic, all of a sudden I had to take blood tests throughout the day. I had to take insulin. Sometimes I have low blood sugar where my body isn't working right and my mind isn't working right. So the strong body and strong mind that I had, now, periodically, are not strong. A few times a week, I experience what I think an Alzheimer's patient experiences. The only difference is I can drink some orange juice and in fifteen or twenty minutes I'm fine. I can vividly remember what it was like to be in a thick fog and not accurately perceive what's happening around me."

Randy cites the apostle Paul's passage from 2 Corinthians 12:7–9: "To keep me from becoming conceited because of these surpassingly great revelations, there was given me a thorn in my flesh, a messenger of Satan, to torment me. Three times I pleaded with the Lord to take it away from me. But he said to me, 'My grace is sufficient for you, for my power is made perfect in weakness.' Therefore I will boast all the more gladly about my weaknesses, so that Christ's power may rest on me."

"I resigned from pastoral ministry, which I loved.

Looking back at it, what God wanted me to do with the rest of my life—I'm convinced that is what I'm doing now," Randy said. "I believe he used the years of pastoral ministry to prepare me for writing, mentoring, and speaking. Because I loved pastoral ministry, I don't think I ever would have stepped away from it. He yanked me away from it.

"Here is an abortion clinic—people whose lives are dedicated to the killing of children, who bring these lawsuits, who bring these writs of garnishment from courts against me, that end up making it necessary that I no longer be a pastor. God used them as God used Joseph's brothers, as Joseph says in Genesis 50:20: 'You meant evil against me, but God meant it for good.'[3] That's exactly what has happened in our lives. I'm so grateful. I would not have it any other way, as hard as those years were."

"God used them as God used Joseph's brothers, as Joseph says in Genesis 50:20: 'You meant evil against me, but God meant it for good.' That's exactly what has happened in our lives."

Randy saw, for instance, that his daughters Karina, then twelve, and Angela, ten, showed courage of their own. Just before the lawsuit went to trial, Lovejoy Surgicenter offered to drop charges against him. He was the only defendant to receive such an offer. The Alcorns held a family meeting to discuss the offer. Randy remembers Karina saying that if

Lovejoy Surgicenter wanted him out of the case, God probably wanted him to remain part of the lawsuit. "She said what I believed in my heart, but I just couldn't say those words to my family. I would have if I'd had to," Randy said. "God graciously allowed my twelve-year-old to say that, and my ten-year-old said, 'Yeah!' She was right there with her sister. Nanci agreed too, as much as she wanted the situation to go away." Randy reminded his daughters that they could lose their house and might have to leave their school. Were they still willing? They nodded. "I get tears in my eyes when I think about it, even now."

"Our daughters, to this day, speak of those days with a sense that they grew," Randy said. "They prayed, and they saw God answer prayers. I think it's very likely, had they not gone through that, they would not be the young women they are, in terms of being sold out to Christ."

TITHING AND TRAINING WHEELS

Being among those penalized for their pro-life protests enabled Randy to do more of what he already wanted to do: scale down his living expenses and give far more money to the kingdom of God. Through Eternal Perspective Ministries, the Alcorns have given away more than $4 million to ministries that engage in evangelism, pro-life and pro-family activism, famine relief, child sponsorship and orphan aid, and activism against human trafficking.

Randy defends tithing against charges of legalism, though he also expresses sadness that some Christians see tithing as the summum bonum of stewardship, rather than the starting place.

Randy defends tithing against charges of legalism, though he also expresses sadness that some Christians see tithing as the summum bonum of stewardship, rather than the starting place. "You'd think it was this extraordinary act of sacrifice and devotion that only great saints would actually give 10 percent. People talk about Old Testament giving and New Testament giving, and one of the greatest misconceptions is that the Old Testament was the tithe, required giving, and New Testament is freewill giving, freewill offering. The Old Testament is *full* of freewill offerings," he said.

"A remarkable number of people, and I've had long conversations with many of them, give absolutely nothing and view the tithe as a legalistic Old Testament thing. To give a tithe would be, to them, like offering an animal sacrifice. It would be ungodly to do it. And of course, they look around and say there are these people who are into tithing as legalism. And there *are* people, absolutely, into tithing as legalism. And I'm completely against that."

Randy explained why God wants more. "What I always say to people is that if you take the standard of 10 percent and say God required it of the poorest people in Old Testament Israel, and now that we're under the grace of Jesus and we have the indwelling Holy Spirit and we live in this incredibly affluent culture, do you think he would expect *less* of us? Does God still have expectations of New Testament people? Clearly he does. In fact, Jesus' message is, 'You have heard that it was said, but I say to you.' And then what does he do each time? He raises the bar.

"New Testament giving—Acts 2 and Acts 4 are very explicit on this—is this contagious liquidating of assets and giving to those in need. How far beyond 10 percent was that? That was taking an already existing asset, liquidating it, and giving the entire thing away. That's giving away 100 percent of that asset, not 100 percent of your income. They gave away what many Christians today, in equivalent terms, might give away over a lifetime, and many would not even give that much."

"New Testament giving—Acts 2 and Acts 4 are very explicit on this—is this contagious liquidating of assets and giving to those in need."

Randy likes to call tithing the training wheels of Christian giving. "The point of putting on training wheels is actually to get you up and get you going to learn how to ride a bike. I think for many Christians tithing can be a very good thing, in that it gets them going on the path of giving in a disciplined way that has some objectivity to it that is measurable," he said. "God's goal is that your life would be lived by the grace of Jesus. Look at 2 Corinthians 8 and 9, the longest New Testament passage on giving, and just study that passage and meditate on it. That's separate from the tithing issue. If you actually capture the spirit of 2 Corinthians 8 and 9 and it becomes a reality in your life, you can forget about tithing."

Not long before I left Randy's home office, our conversation turned to Malachi 3, and especially to God's challenge in verse 10 that the Israelites test him by daring to tithe from their produce. "It's as if God is saying there is something very special about giving. He doesn't say, 'Don't commit adultery. Test me in this. Give *not committing adultery* a try and see if I don't bless you.' God doesn't take his commands and reduce them to the level of 'Oh, give it a try and see if it works.' It's as if he's making a special case out of giving, and he's saying, 'Yes. Test me in this and see if I don't bless you.'

"There's a New Testament equivalent to that. Luke 6:38 is a close parallel to Malachi 3:10, where Jesus says, 'Give, and it will be given to you. A good measure, pressed down, shaken together and running over, will be poured into your lap." Anyone who says, 'Oh, Malachi 3, that's Old Covenant, and it's restricted to that'—no. Luke 6 is very close. 'Watch me abundantly provide for you.' And this is Jesus; this is not King David or Solomon, who are living in splendor. This is Jesus, who doesn't have a rock to lay his head on. He's got the clothes on his back, and not much more. And Jesus is saying, 'Just watch what happens when you give. My heavenly Father is going to overflow.'

> *"Jesus is saying, 'Just watch what happens when you give. My heavenly Father is going to overflow.'"*

"In Malachi, why is that promise there? I think it's because God longs for his people to live the life of grace, to live the life of freewill offering, and see how much fun it is and how God abundantly provides and blesses it."

6

"NEVER TELL ME
WHAT YOU WON'T DO"

Jerald January

As I drove from Chicago's Loop to Vernon Park Church of God on the city's South Side, I knew Jerald January only through the memorable title of his memoir, *A Messed-Up Ride or a Dressed-Up Walk*,[1] and through what I could gather on his church's Web site (www.vpcog.org). In talking with Jerald, I heard heartbreaking stories of casual racism, broken business agreements, and Jerald's sometimes vanquished dreams of promoting a Christian healing that crosses racial barriers. I also heard of perseverance and God's faithfulness, and of how a commitment to tithing has his church on the verge of constructing a spacious new multipurpose campus about sixteen miles south of its current location.

Tragedy struck early in Jerald's life when he saw his

mother fatally shot during a domestic dispute. He remembers hearing the shot and seeing his mother's blood on the kitchen floor. "No one knew I saw her murdered until I was about fourteen years old," he said. "My brothers and I were told that she died in a car accident, but I was there when he shot her. I was a kid, so no one thought that I remembered anything."

Jerald's paternal grandparents took over as his surrogate parents, raising him in inner-city Detroit. The title of his memoir comes from his grandfather's saying that "a messed-up ride is better than a dressed-up walk." He wrote:

> I understood what my grandfather was saying: Let your pride do what it wants to do. You can look great and "dressed-up" and walk to where you need to be, and never get there on time or at all. Or, you can realize that sometimes you're forced to be in circumstances that don't look good to you, but they will get you where you need to be. The ride is "messed up," but at least you're getting there.
>
> Occasionally, though, it is better to have a dressed-up walk. I can't forget what Rosa Parks showed us all. Blacks in Montgomery could have ridden the bus and supported a system that counted them less than human. Instead, they chose to walk to and from church for a full year dressed as domestics, blue-collar workers, and professionals. That dressed-up walk brought a lot of good to the country.[2]

Jerald's book tells of his growing up in Detroit; attending Ferris State College in Big Rapids, Michigan; starting a family in Chicago in the late 1970s and seeing that marriage fail; remarrying in 1985; and working with needy youth in Denver in the early 1990s.

"We lived in a very, very modest house in Detroit. My grandparents and my father raised us. We didn't have a whole lot. My granddad and my grandma believed if you pray and you trust God, he'll let you do anything in the world you want to do," Jerald said. "My grandfather was not allowed to go past sixth grade. He grew up in a town where some of the boys weren't allowed to go past sixth grade because they were black. He said, 'When I was a little boy they told me, "Nigger, you don't need no more education."' He'd always say, 'If I had a high-school diploma, I would have been president of the United States,' because he was such a wise man. To the day he died, he talked about the fact that they never let him go to high school."

Jerald did not face the same severity of obstacles, but he has compiled some broken dreams along the way. A publisher declined to print his next manuscript, *A Second Time*, so he founded his own company, CoolSprings Publishing, Inc.[3] In *A Second Time*, Jerald suggests that the Old Testament prophet Jonah was, to put it plainly, a bigot. "It wasn't a book on reconciliation," he said. "It was a book from a sermon I had preached at Focus on the

Family, which I did only one time. It was something James Dobson was having for denominational leaders. I wanted to talk about the real divisions between blacks and whites in church. That was it. In my study I found that, pretty much, Jonah was a bigot. That's all. He had seen what had happened to his forefathers, and he'd rather die in the ocean than for God to save those people."

A Second Time led to another dashed dream. Jerald appeared on *The 700 Club* to promote the book, and Christian Broadcasting Network subsequently tried to sponsor a conference featuring both Jerald and Jim Cymbala of the Brooklyn Tabernacle. "They based a conference around my book and Jim Cymbala's book on bringing people together from different cultures," he said. "Even though they showed our commercial for thirty days straight, twice on every show, we got a call back saying, 'For the first time in the history of *The 700 Club*, we cannot sell this conference. Our people will not come to hear about blacks and whites loving each other.' They had some great posters. Boy, the artwork was awesome. I was looking forward to doing it, but they said, 'We can't sell it; the people don't want it.'"

Still, one of the most crippling setbacks Jerald experienced was for a touring event he envisioned called the Urban Block Party. "It was a concept God gave me—when the prodigal comes home, kill the fatted calf, and have a big party. We used to have block parties where I grew up—twice a year they block off the neighborhood. But this was like a super show, free of charge to the public. Anybody could come," he said.

Urban Block Party would unite famous athletes from professional football and basketball with actors and singers in a scripted show. Jerald and a partner had lined up corporate sponsorships to cover roughly $93,000 in tour expenses. Then disaster struck. "In a matter of four weeks, my entire life fell apart," Jerald said. "Everything that we had worked for, it just seemed like it had crumbled to dust." One of the tour's major sponsors suddenly backed out of the tour, claiming it had not realized that the majority of its participants were—well, that they were black.

"What? What are you talking about?" Jerald said, looking back at that time. "Eighty-three percent of the NFL is black. We're giving them entrée with the best athletes in the world, and you guys say you love the Lord. It was so close to the event that I didn't have time to get $93,000 together. Everything was booked; it was over the Christmas holidays. I ended up cancelling it. We ate a lot of debt. Some people let us off the hook; some didn't."

Taking the advice of his wife, Jerra, Jerald drove to a secluded retreat center for concentrated prayer. "God didn't say anything to me. I read the Scriptures, and I prayed," Jerald said. "I was saying, 'Just give me a hint. What did I do wrong? Why did this happen like this?' Nothing. On my way home I was stopping to get some gas for my truck, and heard the Holy Spirit whisper, 'Do you love me?' It had to be God, because I wasn't even thinking about God. I was just thinking of how I was going to get out of this debt. I was just pumping gas and said, 'Yeah, Lord, I love you.' Nothing else. About fifteen miles from my exit to go home, I heard the Lord say to me, 'Never tell me what you won't do.' I had told him, 'I will never pastor. Never.'"

> *"I heard the Lord say to me, 'Never tell me what you won't do.'*
> *I had told him, 'I will never pastor. Never.'"*

"I'M THE JOSHUA"

Jerald began preaching at age twenty, but he said that seeing too many wrecked lives of senior pastors had left him resisting the idea of being a senior pastor himself. Ultimately God used the financial collapse of the Urban Block Party to move Jerald toward becoming pastor of Vernon Park Church of God.

"This church had contacted me three times in a year and a half, and I said there was no way in God's green earth that I would pastor a church," he said. "The last thing I wanted to do was pastor a church on the South Side of Chicago. 'Lord, let's not go that way. I live in

Colorado Springs.' Even if I was going to move, I had an offer to go to work for a large Christian businessmen organization, to be a mentor to CFOs and CEOs.

"As much as I didn't want to pastor, I knew God wanted me here. I didn't tell them that, though. They asked me to come here and speak at a meeting for young people. It was in the spring of 1999, in the week after the Lord had spoken to me. I wasn't going to pastor, but I thought, *Lord, if I at least go and preach, maybe you'll ease up off me a little bit.* I came and spoke on a Sunday morning. They only had one service then, with about two hundred members. It was just a common service, to me. I wasn't particularly good, and it wasn't a particularly good service. But from Monday to Thursday, every night I spoke, more and more people came. By Thursday it was standing room only, and people were standing in the hallways. One trustee said, 'We haven't had this in years.' My wife leaned over to me and said, 'I think God's setting us up.'"

Soon afterward Jerald accepted the church's offer, but only as an interim pastor. "After about a year, I thought, *Okay, maybe I'm supposed to be here.* I never let them install me as the pastor, though. I was the pastor, but we never had any installation services. I signed a one-year contract. I figured they may not like me, and I might not like them. I love God, but I know enough guys fail at this thing. I was coming into a church that, even though it's prestigious, it was not very healthy financially. It was a nice building, but it had problems."

Jerald said he made a deal with God: if, within a year, the church grew from 200 people to about 350, and if tithes and offerings increased, he would stay. He was not, he stressed, paid on commission. By the next February, the church had grown from 230 to about 300. "The church was getting healthier; the offerings went up $2,000 or $3,000 a Sunday. We were able to pay off some bills," he said. "Someone asked me, 'Why did you do it that way?' There are about six million people in Cook County. If I can't attract 350 of them, I'm not the guy for the job. I have other skills. I can go do something else."

Jerald is the second pastor of Vernon Park Church of God, which Claude and Addie Wyatt founded in a garage in 1955. "I'm the Joshua," Jerald said.

A TURNING POINT IN TITHING

A turning point in the congregation's life came when Jerald began teaching a class called "Right Relationship to Wealth" on Wednesday nights. "I wanted people to understand what the Bible really says about money. People told me, 'We have never heard this like this before. You made it so plain.'"

Trustees told Jerald that offerings shot up from $7,500 a week to $11,000 a week. "Some people put little notes in [the collection basket] saying they had never understood what tithing was. Some people even went back as far as a year and made up every tithe they had missed. I had never told anyone to do anything like that. I really never believed that the offering should be a big part of the service." The offering now lasts only a few minutes, and Jerald jokes that it occurs just before the benediction, so people can withhold their offerings if the sermon annoyed them.

Membership in the church has continued growing. Vernon Park now has about eleven hundred members. For a time, the church expanded its schedule to three services on Sunday. Jerald said he found that schedule too exhausting, and he scaled back to two services. With that growth has come a sense of outgrowing Vernon Park's current facility. Jerald believes he heard the Lord say to him, "Build me a house."

"I thought, *Okay, Lord, we'll build another church.* As my studies went on, I sensed he wasn't just talking about building a church. As I was reading the words of Jesus, 'In my Father's house are many mansions,'[4] I had this concept about a campus, a holistic campus where we not only have a church but also have a place for a seniors building, an athletic building, maybe twelve or thirteen acres."

Eventually a member of Jerald's church spotted land

in Lynwood, Illinois, owned by the survivors of an immigrant farmer. The member knocked on the farmhouse door, introduced himself, and explained that his pastor had a vision for a multipurpose campus. Jerald was hoping to find land at about $135,000 an acre, compared to prices ranging between $190,000 and $500,000 elsewhere in Cook County. He heard from the family's attorney that the survivors were willing to sell the property to Vernon Park—if the church was willing to buy all forty-three acres of the farm.

"It was a whole-faith thing," Jerald said. "I told God, 'Okay, God, we're a tithing church; we give. We even tithe off of what people give us to other ministries around the country and around the world. But we're not a big church. We're what we call a tweener church—we're too big to be small, too small to be big.'"

When trustees from the church met with family members, at first Jerald could not believe the price was as low as it was: $18,000 an acre. "They said, 'Pastor, this makes absolutely no sense. We got there, and there was no negotiation. The owner just said, 'If the church shows up, offer them the land for this amount of money.' I said, 'Guys, this is $18,000 an acre. The houses across the street—four houses per acre—start at $400,000.' It just didn't make any sense to me. I said, 'This is great: $637,000 for forty-three acres of prime land on a main street half a block from the expressway. Something's wrong—Jimmy Hoffa's buried on it—*something*.' My faith should have been better than that, but it wasn't."

At the closing, the youngest of the farmer's three daughters began crying.

Asking her sisters' permission, she told the story of their parents, who came to this country as immigrant sharecroppers. The farmer asked God for his own land, praying that if God would grant that dream, "he would use it to God's glory and be a secret tither to ministries all over the world," Jerald said. "No one would ever know, but he would make God proud that he gave him that land. In Lynwood this old man was famous, because his rows were so straight. He didn't have the best equipment, but everybody knew how much he loved God. She said, 'Papa taught us how to pray, walking through the corn out there on that land.'"

Jerald sees further significance in the purchase. In the early years of the farm's life, blacks weren't allowed to live in that southern part of Cook County. It was Ku Klux Klan territory.

In time the church acquired still another thirty-five acres, at the same price per acre, from a neighbor who was the farmer's best friend for many years. Ultimately, the church bought just over seventy-five acres of land for a bit more than $1 million.

Jerald's plan for the property, which will be called Vernon Park Village, comprises twenty-two acres for the church and offices; forty-four acres for housing, especially retirement condos; and on the front end, mostly retail and commercial, with one corner of luxury rentals for retired people.

Jerald is confident the church will retain a ministry to needy people in its new location. "Less than a mile from us is the poorest neighborhood in the state of Illinois, Ford Heights. Our missions ministry for the church is already putting together programs—not just food programs, but education programs for the children. We're already meeting with four different school boards in that area. We're looking forward to it. There's a trailer park less than a quarter of a mile from where we are."

Jerald said that tithing has been a guiding principle throughout his Christian life, and he has suffered when he strayed from it. He credits his grandparents with teaching him about tithing. "They always went to church. My grandmother was a Baptist, and my grandfather was a Methodist. No matter whose church we went to, the offering plate never went by unless they put money in it. They made us put money in. They gave us money, and that quarter could buy a lot of penny candy. That wasn't odd to us. They were always blessed. They weren't well-educated people, but they were always blessed," he said.

Jerald said that tithing has been a guiding principle throughout his Christian life, and he has suffered when he strayed from it.

"I have seen what happens when you don't tithe, in my own life, twice. I had become, for some reason, a tither of convenience. If things were going okay, I convinced myself that I could skip it this time. I remember having a house foreclosed. I had to apologize to my wife, because I knew it was my fault. I don't know where I picked up that habit, but somewhere in my late twenties and early thirties I was doing that, and I filed for bankruptcy and everything. From that day to this day, we have not ceased to tithe, plus give 5 percent in offerings, on everything that we own. Everything. It's been twenty-one years. I don't care if I was unemployed or not. I don't care what it was from. We always do that. We've never needed anything. We've never gone hungry. We tell people that we believe that same mantle has fallen on our church."

7

DEEP GLADNESS MEETS DEEP HUNGER

Kevin Jones

IN OCTOBER 2002, REPORTER KEVIN JONES WROTE
about "Confessing the Faith," a national conference of
conservative activists within mainline Protestant churches.
Kevin's report left no doubt about which side he was on.
He opposed these conservatives, but he also expressed a
grudging respect for their perseverance. "From what I've
seen, they are playing a deeply sophisticated and subtle
game and playing it in a relentless and patient style, determined to take the time it takes to win," he wrote in an
online article. "Are progressives playing at that level? Are
we willing to?"[1]

Kevin and his wife, the Reverend Rosa Lee Harden,
immersed themselves for a time in the culture wars of the
Episcopal Church. They launched a popular Web site,

Every Voice Network, which offered original reporting and frequent commentary. By 2004 they developed a multi-media curriculum, Via Media, which used many of the techniques (video content followed by small-group discussions over dinner) of the Alpha course, a popular introduction to the Christian faith. Via Media's theology was considerably different, though: while Alpha flows from the charismatic and evangelical stream of Anglicanism, Via Media flows from the liberal stream.

Kevin was a force to be reckoned with, and a somewhat intimidating one at that. Drawing on his years of experience as a reporter of both religion and business news, Kevin delved into public records that established connections between conservative activist groups and wealthy benefactors. A few of the headlines from Kevin's stories during the Episcopal Church's General Convention of 2003 convey what a happy warrior he was: "Anglican Imperialism: How the AAC [American Anglican Council] Funds International Allies," "[Gene] Robinson Controversy: Allegations Weak, Timing Suspicious," "Conservatives Plot Next Steps."[2]

Still, one of the things I most remember from that General Convention was when reporters stood in line for more than an hour, waiting for the seats allotted to us when the House of Bishops would debate whether to approve of Gene Robinson as the first Episcopal Church bishop who spoke openly of his gay partner before his election was approved. As reporters stood by, fighting away boredom with occasional small talk, Kevin walked along the line, offering free bottles of water. "I'll take one," I said, marking the first time I spoke with him. This was an almost inconsequential moment, but it also was a glimpse of Kevin as something more than a happy warrior.

I saw more of this side of both Kevin and Rosa Lee in May 2004, when I traveled to Jackson, Mississippi, to learn more about their Via Media curriculum. I attended as a reporter rather than a subscriber of the curriculum, and I wanted to interview the publishers about their vision and their goals. After a daylong training session, Kevin and I chatted by a hotel pool while Rosa Lee worked in some therapeutic swimming. Kevin and Rosa Lee invited me to join them and several other friends for a meal at a Red Hot & Blue restaurant, a barbecue chain in which the late conservative firebrand Lee Atwater made an early investment. Among those who have lived in the South, eating barbecue together covers a multitude of conflicts. What I remember most about that evening was riding back to the hotel with Kevin and Rosa Lee after dinner. We took a few detours so they could drive past homes they had helped build as part of Habitat for Humanity in Jackson.

They spoke fondly of their involvement with Habitat, a time they used not only to build houses but also to broaden the Jackson chapter's vision of long-term community transformation.

"Maybe we should do a better job of quantifying the economic costs of poverty to get folks in," Kevin said. "That's a lot of what Rosa Lee did with Habitat in Jackson, to get people involved. It wasn't that you wanted to just care about housing for poor folks, but she could talk about lower policing costs, lower social-service costs, higher property taxes, higher economic-development quotients—oh, and poor folks get houses, and the percentage of them that finish high school is so much greater. You have to find a way to sell good to people with small hearts. It's a continual challenge."

"You have to find a way to sell good to people with small hearts. It's a continual challenge."

As I think back on those years of Every Voice Network and Via Media, it becomes clear that even then Kevin wanted to do more than take sides in the Episcopal Church's vigorous but often circular debates. Even in 2002, when he took on the Association for Church Renewal, his online biography included this paragraph: "He is currently working toward building a community that will re-vision the roles of business and capitalism. Read more about that budding work at collectiveintelligence.net."[3]

I visited the Collective Intelligence Web site on occasion, but I found it a bit heavy on Web jargon and contemporary economic theory. I noticed that Kevin had become involved in the Anglican Malaria Project, and I wrote him once to say I missed his voice in our shared church's debates—mostly because of his willingness to step back from the battle on occasion and comment on the power struggles on both sides. Kevin wrote back to say he was feeling too fulfilled in his work with Good Capital, LLC (www.goodcapital.net), to be very tempted by church politics.

I asked Kevin to tell me more about Good Capital, and we agreed that an in-person interview in San Francisco was a good idea. Kevin and Rosa Lee live in a modest-sized and eco-friendly apartment in the Noe Valley neighborhood. Good Capital's office is within walking distance, and so is Rosa Lee's church, Holy Innocents, which has about two hundred members.

HOLISTIC GENEROSITY

Kevin and Rosa Lee tithe, but Kevin thinks of tithing as too modest a goal for stewardship. "I think we have a responsibility with our resources. It's more like the talents parable: what did we do with what came our way?" he said. "Tithing seems like an obligation, whereas the parable of the talents seems like a relationship, a transaction, a gift, and return of that gift. That makes more sense to me."

"I think we have a responsibility with our resources. It's more like the talents parable: what did we do with what came our way?"

As a Silicon Valley entrepreneur, Kevin built one company, Net Market Makers, to $18 million in revenues, and sold it for $30 million in early 2000. Kevin demurs about how much of his wealth he will invest in Good Capital as one of its three principals, but the company intends to invest $1 million to $3 million per deal in ten to twelve enterprises. Good Capital says the company also will seek investments from "high-net-worth individuals, religious capital, and foundations."[4]

Kevin said Good Capital wants to challenge the traditional approach to philanthropy, which he sees as an inadequate and miserly response to a world in need. Kevin believes that Andrew Carnegie's two "Gospel of Wealth" essays, first published by *North American Review* in 1889, sold Americans on a philosophy that treated the market as a force of nature best left unregulated. "Philanthropy is so completely emasculated that 95 percent of a foundation is built on a capital-management vehicle and it has a 5 percent donation arm out the back," he said. "That's really what foundations are. They only have to distribute 5 percent of their corpus every year toward their product or their service. That's being dethroned in a radical and big and good way by something called mission-related investing. There are some big foundations driving it but also some smaller, catalytic foundations driving it—the F. B. Heron Foundation, the Meyer Memorial Trust, and the Annie E. Casey Foundation, where they want at least 2 percent of that 95 percent to be invested in line with the mission."

When a philanthropic foundation gives away only 5 percent of its corpus in a year, "philanthropy is in this little encapsulated bubble. The way we think about our money, we have two pockets. We have the investment pocket and a little bitty giving pocket. That's allowed by a thing called externalities," he said. "There are two areas of externalities: environmental and social. Global warming has put the environment on the balance sheet, so it's no longer an externality. It's a cost that's being factored in by every business. The reinsurance companies are asking insurance companies, 'What's the exposure of this business to global warming or other climate change?' Poverty, unfortunately, is not on the balance sheet, so it's still an externality. When Wal-Mart externalizes the cost of health care to the state by not paying benefits, it can maximize profits, but it doesn't mean that there's not a social cost. We're bearing that cost, but we allow corporations to do that."

Good Capital also works against an assumption that foundations need to think about the social good only when making grants. He cites a series of articles by the *Los Angeles Times* that said the Bill and Melinda Gates Foundation, in the *Times*'s words, "reaps vast financial gains every year from investments that contravene its good works."[5]

"There's a complete dichotomy from the investment side of the house, where they say they have a fiduciary responsibility, a legal responsibility, to grow the corpus and so they can't think about mission. Mission is just out the back. It's kind of the wrong end of the horse, as my friend Jed Emerson [a lecturer at the Stanford School of Business] says. That series of articles is causing a huge move, basically, to say, 'Do we have a Gates Foundation exposure in our portfolio?'" Kevin said.

"It's a deeper level of stewardship. It means asking, 'What is my money doing to the planet and to the people?'"

"I don't walk to talk about philanthropy. I want to talk about you and your assets and what you want to do with them in the world. We're raising a fund where it's on the line between giving and investing. You don't just look at risk and return, but you look at risk and return and your impact. It's a deeper level of stewardship. It means asking, 'What is my money doing to the planet and to the people?' I think that's what we're responsible for. If we use philanthropy, we're using old, outdated cultural frames that lock us into the doctrine that was laid down by Andrew Carnegie. We want to dethrone the current myths of capital. We think it's a devil's bargain, and the times are such that we have to do it. The planet demands it, and the people demand it."

Good Capital does not want to limit its definition of responsible investment to as narrow a category as fair trade. Kevin said that concept has become so broad as to be almost meaningless. "We're looking to invest in fair-trade companies that offer a living wage all the way down but are organic all the way down. It's really interesting: You can't get a premium for fair trade, because if you say *fair trade* you just reach the Birkenstock kind of hippie crowd, the pity crowd—you can be in your caftans and buy your fair trade caftans. Some of these folks aren't using the words *fair trade* anymore. They want to get beyond that. They're calling it *sustainable sourcing*. It's environmentally sound and socially sound. There's an old formulation of things like fair trade that people are starting to get beyond, in terms of crafts and artisanal things. In coffee, fair trade is asking, 'Is it organic? Is it shade-grown? Is it fair trade?' Well, Sam's Club can do that, so they're moving in there."

Kevin mentions two examples of the kinds of business in which Good Capital plans to invest: Evergreen Lodge and Better World Books. Kevin personally invested in

Evergreen Lodge as a startup, and Good Capital announced in April 2008 that it would provide Better World Books with up to $2.5 million in growth capital.

Evergreen Lodge (www.evergreenlodge.com) is a bed-and-breakfast on the west side of Yosemite National Park that also trains at-risk young people as season interns. "A third of their population consists of people from halfway houses, young men and women," Kevin said. "There's a cost to the intake of those folks. You have to find the right ones who can learn a career in a hotel or restaurant. There are social workers on staff, as well as kids from the ghetto who have never been to the Sierras. It has a huge impact. They're working around college kids, who have always had a different set of options and hopes than kids from the ghettos, so that causes a change. And then there's outplacement to hotels that have learned to work with them. There's a hard cost to that. It's about $300,000 to $400,000 a year in hard costs, and there are some soft costs. 'At-risk' means there's some risk with these kids. They don't have work habits. They haven't been in a supervised situation with positive goals before, a lot of them. But it still makes 12 percent. There's a subsidization of a social mission inside a for-profit business."

Better World Books sells both new and used books, and many of its used books come from both college campuses and libraries. At the top of its online store (www.betterworldbooks.com), Better World keeps tallies of how many used books it has kept out of landfills and how much money it has contributed to help spread literacy across the world. Better World offers the customary shipping options, from standard to urgent, but it uses Carbonfund.org to make its shipments carbon-neutral.

"The reason we got to them, and not another fund, is that they wanted to give away more than any other investor would deal with," Kevin said of Better World Books. "They wanted to give away 10 percent top line. We said that's not going to work. You can give away 5 percent top line and give 5 percent of your stock to your nonprofit literacy partners— Room to Read, Books for Africa, based on their performance. Our investors will give up 5 percent of that return that we could have gotten, and you give up 5 percent of your company, and we can strike a deal. That's the thing we did, and we will report every year on the pounds of books that didn't go to the landfill because they were sold online, the tons of carbon offset because they ship carbon-neutral, and then the number of books that go to the literacy groups."

A LONG SEARCH FOR JUSTICE

In describing the spiritual aspect of his work with Good Capital, Kevin reached for an observation by essayist and novelist Frederick Buechner. Rosa Lee helped him recall how Buechner defines *vocation* in his book *Wishful Thinking: A Seeker's ABC*: "The place God calls you to is the place where your deep gladness and the world's deep hunger meet."[6]

"I am finding more meaning in my everyday tasks, which has a spiritual dimension. There's the impact I know we're having on people's lives with the companies we're investing in, and yet we're doing it with a level of professional skill that took me thirty-five years of my life to acquire," he said. "I'm bringing more of myself to it, as opposed to just my professional self. I can talk about what things really mean and why we're doing it and why we should bear the cost of doing good. This is a load our capital should carry.

"I am finding more meaning in my everyday tasks, which has a spiritual dimension. There's the impact I know we're having on people's lives with the companies we're investing in."

"I can talk to my kids in a different way. My kids are pretty much fringe left, permaculture farmers in intentional communities. I can talk about the impact I'm trying to have on the world in a way that makes sense to them. That's really important. I couldn't do that while I was in business. I get no satisfaction out of traditional business anymore. I know how to do it, but it's a game that is empty to me. I can bring my whole self to this in a way that I've never brought my whole self to business before. We've had things where I did good *over here* and I did business *over there*. This is a unifying thing that breaks down the compartmentalization that I had to live within when I was in traditional business."

Kevin has explored ways to help the poor for much of his life. "I became a Christian in 1970 via the Jesus Movement. They asked me to open my heart, and that scared me to death. I thought I was with some bloodletting cult," he said. "I lived in a house with other converts through college and went to Southern Baptist seminary to work with poor folks. I discovered I did not have the temperament to be a community activist."

He worked with the Anglican Malaria Project, but that, too, became a lesson in what sort of work he's equipped to do. "We discovered that well-meaning entrepreneurial white folks coming in with a great solution in Mozambique had so much to learn," he said. "It was a great learning enterprise. I learned that I am much better at being an advocate than I am in on-the-ground direct service with the level of incremental change that happens with really poor folks in Africa. A fast-moving entrepreneur is not the same profile as a community organizer. I worked on it for two years. We set up a great system, and then I realized I wasn't the person to push it forward."

Kevin traces his passion for helping the poor to his growing up in a working-class home. "We were the single blue-collar, financially challenged family within a larger, white-collar, affluent family. My father repaired washing machines. The uncles who were doctors and lawyers cut the turkey at Thanksgiving. We got the meat they didn't want, down at the end of the table. That got pointed out to them at one dinner. They informed my father and mother that all was right with the world and we'd continue to be down at the foot of the table. That made me aware that simply speaking about injustice to those in power or those with money did not cause them to change.

"Even asking did not change the basic power structures. My first tactic, which I employed half a dozen times, was to become one of the guys at the head of the table," he said. "But after doing that several times, I realized my heart was with the people down at the foot of the table. I was over fifty before I realized that becoming rich and powerful was not really much of an answer, that working to restructure the capital markets, and business, and the way people think about power and money, was at the heart of what I want my life to be about."

8

A SENSE OF COMMUNITY

Mark Kellner

When my fellow journalist Mark Kellner agreed to discuss tithing with me, we met at an open-air mall in downtown Silver Spring, Maryland, and then made our way to a Thai restaurant. It was a slightly chilly Saturday night in mid-September. When I first met Mark in early 2000, we got together at a P. F. Chang's at Fashion Island, another open-air mall, in Newport Beach, California. I suppose that if Mark and I have a serendipitous final meeting just before we die, or before the Second Coming of Christ, it will be at a Mongolian barbecue in a city yet to be determined. Mark and I came to know each other because we're both journalists with a particular fondness for writing about religion. From the moment I first spoke to Mark regarding this book, he emphasized that he would speak only for himself and not for any past or current church or employer. I agreed to make that clear.

His pilgrimage through the American religious landscape is offbeat, if not even exotic. First, the bird's-eye
view: Jewish childhood, teenage years with the Worldwide
Church of God, seventeen years as a member of the
Salvation Army, and now more than ten years as a member of the Seventh-day Adventist Church. His interest in
American religions is not merely journalistic. In most of
the changes in his chosen places of worship—except for a
three-year respite at Marble Collegiate Church, the home
of Norman Vincent Peale's gospel of positive thinking—
Mark has committed himself to churches that make no
small demands of their members.

"I find it interesting to see people who make a commitment and who stick to it—especially when that commitment
is sort of countercultural and when it can involve real sacrifice," Mark said. To complement this thought, Mark tells
the joke about the respective sacrifices that a hen and a pig
make so a farmer may have a breakfast of eggs and bacon.
You probably know the punch line: the pig turns to the
hen and says, "You're making a commitment. I'm making
a sacrifice."

*"I find it interesting to see people who make a commitment and
who stick to it—especially when that commitment is sort of
countercultural and when it can involve real sacrifice."*

A CONVERSION INTERRUPTED

If Mark were handling this transition sentence, he might frame it as a joke: "How did a nice Jewish boy from Queens wind up in a church like this?" It's a long story, but this narrative will hit the highlights.

"I figured out at a very early age who the Messiah was," Mark said. "I was playing hooky one day from school, and Billy Graham was on the television. Now, there was no warning, there was no crawl along the bottom of the screen that said, 'Warning! Jewish people do not need to watch this!' And so I watched, and what Billy Graham said made sense. It made a lot of sense. This was shortly before my thirteenth birthday. My folks came home and I said, 'Guess what? I'm a Christian.' And they said, 'Guess what? You're not.' At the age of thirteen, in the Jewish tradition, one is confirmed in a bar mitzvah as an adult member of the faith. My parents were in the process of spending what was, for those days, a very handsome sum of money—thousands of dollars. They essentially suppressed my Christianity then. I went along. I was a little changeable then, although obviously something stuck in the back of my mind."

By 1975, Mark joined Herbert W. Armstrong's Worldwide Church of God.[1] At the time the Worldwide Church of God—Mark calls it simply the Worldwide Church—practiced a multilayered approach to tithing that made a mandatory 10 percent look like child's play. "In the Worldwide Church, tithing was mandated very strongly," Mark said. "You had your first tithe, which was 10 percent off the top, sent in to the headquarters in Pasadena. There was a second tithe, which was to be retained by the member, and—every three years after baptism—a third tithe, which also went to headquarters. Ostensibly that third tithe was for the care of widows and orphans in the church. In actuality, those who were critical of Herbert Armstrong suggested that among the widows and orphans was a Grumman Gulfstream II jet, and that some of the widows may have been young lady friends of Garner Ted Armstrong, who was ousted during my association with the Worldwide Church."

Mark expressed a fondness for how the Worldwide Church advised its members to spend their second tithe: "The second tithe, that was kind of a brilliant thing. This was all from Leviticus, of course. The second tithe was meant to defray your expenses at the church's annual camp meeting called the Feast of Tabernacles—ten days, usually in a resort area of some stripe or another. You went away from home, you saved up your money, and you went to town—not riotously, not in debauchery, per se. You basically went out and you had a good time. It was supposed to be a foretaste of heaven. You know, I like that."

Other than the second tithe, however, most of what

Worldwide Church members gave supported the work of their headquarters—and a widely reported lavish lifestyle favored by its founder. "Of course, there were suggestions," Mark said. "For example, as you were planning for the festival, the suggestion was to send in a *tithe of the tithe* to maintain the assembly halls and campgrounds and meeting places that the church did own. They didn't own local buildings, but they would have these regional places to gather. There was pressure, shall we say, to contribute festival offerings, and reasonably healthy ones at that. Armstrong's view was that we were in the gun lap toward the end of everything, so why get your teeth fixed? Give money to the work."

Looking back, Mark does not resent the Worldwide Church's higher-than-average sense of tithing. "I was a kid; I was a teenager. Herbert Armstrong spent $10 million building one of the finest auditoriums on the West Coast, the Ambassador Auditorium in Pasadena. There's $20 of mine somewhere in there, but in the perspective of history it's not a whole lot," Mark said. Instead, Mark left the Worldwide Church less because of its rigorous demands on tithing but because he was disenchanted by how poorly he believed Herbert Armstrong treated his family members and subordinates. "What did trouble me toward the end, and what has always troubled me in observing tithing situations or situations involving church finance, is when you treat the people below you worse than you take care of yourself. Herbert did that with just about everyone he came into contact with, including his children."

Mark said little about his time with Marble Collegiate Church, except to offer this compliment for how that church handled its stewardship messages: "Every fall they did something that made an impression on me and that I wish more churches would do.

"On a series of Sunday mornings, people would come up and give a testimony about their commitment to tithe and what that did for them."

"Every fall, [Marble Collegiate Church] did something that made an impression on me and that I wish more churches would do. On a series of Sunday mornings, people would come up and give a testimony about their commitment to tithe and what that did for them."

Mark does not say a great deal more about the Salvation Army, but its hymnody and theology left a lasting impression. "The battle within the Salvation Army, very briefly, is whether they're going to end up as primarily or largely a social services agency or whether they're going to remain true to their evangelical roots. William Booth was very concerned about evangelism, and social service evolved as a way to get the gospel to people. The idea was not just to go around and do good works and set up canteens at house fires. The idea was to win people for Christ."

Mark said his tithing was less consistent during his years with Marble Collegiate Church and the Salvation Army. "We have all sorts of wonderful choruses in the Salvation Army. One is 'I am not under law but under grace / It was grace that rescued me / It was grace that set me free / I have sought, I have found the hiding place / I am not under law but under grace.' When the budget was tight, I would sort of turn to that, and to a companion chorus from the Salvation Army: 'Grace there is my every debt to pay / Blood to wash my every sin away / Power to keep me spotless day by day / For me, for me.'"

BECOMING ADVENTISTS

Mark said his attraction to Adventism occurred when he and his wife had hit a plateau in their experience with the Salvation Army. "One day, I was listening to the radio and I heard a commercial for a fellow who was giving a series of public lectures. I happened to know that the fellow was a Seventh-day Adventist. I also knew that my wife was not overly favorable toward Seventh-day Adventism. In order to get her to go to these lectures, I did what any self-respecting husband would do in a similar situation: I told her only half the truth. I said, 'Listen, here's a guy who's going to give these lectures on Bible archaeology, on the pyramids, on the pharaohs.' And he *was* doing this. She agreed to go, and we kept going. We accepted the Seventh-day Adventist message. I was baptized as a Seventh-day Adventist in April 1999. My wife was baptized a couple of weeks later."

Beneath the frequent asides and a delivery akin to Jackie Mason's, Mark is serious about his faith. He commits himself to a church that celebrates its Christian Sabbath on Saturday, urges its members to abide by a vegetarian diet, and teaches this on tithing: "God's plan for the support of His work on this earth is through the tithe and freewill offerings of His people. The tithe is the main source of funding for the total proclamation of the gospel to all the world by the Seventh-day Adventist Church."[2]

The Seventh-day Adventist Church says much more than this about tithing, of course. Its "Guidelines on the Use of Tithe" run just over sixteen hundred words, laying down strict rules for how Adventist leaders are to distribute the tithes they collect and where they collect them (within their own geographical conferences or divisions).[3]

"We talk in the church about people 'returning tithes' because we believe, as the Bible says, that 'the earth is the LORD's, and the fullness thereof.'"

Mark questions whether the tithe is a biblical requirement, but he trusts his church's teaching about its importance in supporting the church. Mark uses an

Adventist phrase—to *return tithe*—when referring to his giving. "We talk in the church about people 'returning tithes' because we believe, as the Bible says, that 'the earth is the LORD's, and the fullness thereof,'"[4] he said. "If everything belongs to him, if he owns the cattle on a thousand hills, I don't own the cattle but I get to use them. I'm returning to God what he has given me."

So, then, Mark returns tithes. "I have no problem with adhering to and supporting the church's position. I do find things in Scripture and in history that raise questions. Tithing was to be done on agricultural goods. As far as I know, there's no mention in Scripture of tithing on money. There are scriptures where it is sort of implied or where you can *infer* something—such as when Paul talks about setting aside on the first day of the week an offering.[5] But Paul, who would certainly have known the custom of tithing from his Pharisaical training, did not say, 'On the first day of the week, get your tithe ready.' Was it a special offering? Was it something else? Were offerings meant to be something one gives from money, and the tithe was from agricultural produce? Let's face it: one of the things people in my denomination are accused of is legalism. I don't really think that those who are truly Christian at heart within our denomination are legalists. I do not observe the Sabbath to get to heaven, however imperfectly I may or may not observe it. I do it out of love. And I do

it because I read the fourth commandment fairly literally,
I guess."

BELONGING TO THE BODY OF CHRIST

Mark also affirms tithing because it gives a sense of belonging to some larger body of Christians, some larger purpose
other than personal fulfillment.

"Community is important, and I believe going to
church is important. Now, how do I apply this to tithing? I
have experienced this very keenly, both in Seventh-day
Adventism and in the Salvation Army. When you join a
church of that nature—in one sense, particularly with the
Salvation Army, you are part of an international community. I have been in Japan. I was in Kobe after the Hengchun
earthquake, and we were in a tiny little Salvation Army
building. There were some Japanese Salvation Army offi-
cers, myself, and other people from the United States. We
all sat around the same table. We had the same hymns.
They were singing in Japanese; we were singing in English.
There's a sense of community there.

"As a Seventh-day Adventist, I have been in Nairobi,
Kenya, where I have been the only Caucasian person in a
congregation of one thousand people renting an audito-
rium at the University of Nairobi. They were singing

mostly in Swahili. I was trying to sing in Swahili because they had the hymnal in front of me. When I was in the city of Kaunas in Lithuania, and we were all together singing Jack Hayford's song 'Majesty,' they were singing in Lithuanian, and I was singing in English. You feel a part of a larger fellowship than you do otherwise," he said. "Tithing is a similar thing. By contributing and being a part financially of the church at the local level, the district level, the regional level, the national level, and the world level—because the tithe money in our denomination flows upward—it's a great linking thing."

Creating a sense of connection is important in helping church members know they belong in a community and in encouraging them to stay in that community. "We've got tons of people coming into the church through the front door of the church, and we're grateful for it. Sometimes we will lose some of them through the back door because they haven't been nurtured properly or they don't feel connected for some other reason. That's why I believe connection is important," Mark said.

"When you decide to become a Seventh-day Adventist, you have to be pretty hard-core. If you're going to rearrange your life in that fashion, I would like to see someone stay committed to it. Now if they elect to leave, I wish them Godspeed and pray they'd return and reconsider, but I'm not trying to imprison people. I want people to be happy doing what they're doing, and I want them to be happy being a part of the fellowship. That's where the connection comes in. I think there's value in going to a church every week, going to a building that is not your home, that is not your familiar surroundings, and coming together with other people. The Scripture says do not forsake the assembling of yourselves together.[6] I don't know of too many people who leave a church or a community or a faith group where they're happy."

Mark sees tithing as both expressing and creating a deeper sense of connection with each other and with God. "It is a way of establishing a bond that you wouldn't have otherwise. By being in that channel, if you will, being in that mind-set, I certainly think that God is more able to show favor in a way that we recognize it. Strictly speaking, if you really want to get Talmudic about it, every moment in our lives is an incredible gift from God. I know from my own circumstances that there has been more than one occasion where I should have been dead, a long time ago. God has elected to keep me alive, to a certain point. I've heard it said that we are immortal until we have completed the mission that God has given us," he said.

"I wouldn't want to deny it to the people who well and truly need this for whatever reason, but you can essentially turn on your television any Sunday morning and go to church, and have almost every element of a church service except maybe the guy snoring next to you. And you send in your offering to the television preacher, and all is well. But that kind of sterility and that kind of being in a silo, if you will, I find very troubling. It's better when you smash the silo and you become a part of a community. I'm borrowing a metaphor from the IT industry, where data has been kept in all these compartments, silos, and the whole idea now is to smash everything and let all the information mix. When you get people out of their shells and into the community, that's where the miracles happen."

"When you get people out of their shells and into the community, that's where the miracles happen."

9

"THE ESSENCE OF GOD IS ALWAYS TO BE GIVING"

Ed Bacon

IN THE MID-1990S, AS PART OF MY WORK FOR A CONSER-vative activist group within the Episcopal Church, I began reporting on the annual conference of the Association of Diocesan Liturgy and Music Commissions (ADLMC). One thing stands out from ADLMC's annual meetings: hearing a message by the Reverend J. Edwin Bacon Jr. for the first time. Ed was fairly new as rector of All Saints in Pasadena, one of the best-known liberal congregations in the Episcopal Church.

What was most memorable about Ed's talk had little to do with liturgy or music. Rather, he described a congregation that calls its members to give. Ed told how he would host new parishioners at his home and urge them to become involved in one of the parish's plethora of service-oriented groups—including COLORS (Christians Offering Love to Overcome Racism in Society), GAIA (the Global AIDS Interfaith Alliance), and Night Basketball and Books, which helps low-income children and adolescents.

Almost as an aside, he mentioned that All Saints encourages its members to tithe. Ed's talk caught me by surprise. Given my assumptions about this congregation, and given the standard topics of ADLMC addresses, I had expected little more than political bromides and perhaps a peacock-like display of liturgical novelties. Ed's talk brought me up short. I thought, *Here is a liberal congregation spreading a gospel that makes some demands on your soul and on your time. Here is a place where you will not be praised effusively just for showing up on Sunday morning.*

When Ed concluded his remarks at ADLMC, I walked forward to thank him. In the ten-plus years since then, I've always enjoyed seeing Ed. We are usually on opposite sides of our shared denomination's political and theological divides. What we share is a sense that those questions matter. If you're an activist within the church long enough, you befriend people on the other side of your favorite questions—or you avoid becoming friends with them. Life is richer when Ed Bacon is your friend.

Knowing of Ed's emphasis on tithing added a sense of poignancy to news reports involving the congregation's conflict with the Internal Revenue Service. All Saints caught the unblinking eye of the IRS after its previous rector, the Reverend George F. Regas, preached a sermon two days before the presidential election of 2004. George did not endorse either major candidate, but he did imagine Jesus saying to George W. Bush, "Mr. President, your doctrine of preemptive war is a failed doctrine. Forcibly changing the regime of an enemy that posed no imminent threat has led to disaster."

In June 2005, All Saints received an IRS letter saying that its tax-exempt status could be revoked because of that sermon's political content. One thing was clear, even from a distance: the IRS chose its target poorly. All Saints retained a Washington law firm to fight the investigation until the agency backed down. The IRS backed down in September 2007, saying it had concluded that the church had "intervened in the 2004 Presidential election campaign" but adding, "We note that this was a one-time occurrence and that you have policies in place to ensure that the Church complies with the prohibition against intervention in campaigns for public office."

"There was never any doubt about the course that we were going to take," Ed said over breakfast in a hotel restaurant adjacent to All Saints. "We always knew that we were going to fight this. We knew it was unjust, in the first place. If we had to fight to the Supreme Court, we would do that. If the Supreme Court ruled against us, we would continue on with our identity. Nobody ever blinked an eye about that."

For his part, George also was clear that no IRS investigation—or even a revocation of tax-exempt status—would affect the parish clergy's collective will to address political questions from the pulpit. "That congregation is so profoundly committed to being a prophetic church, to trying speak truth to power and all that means, and they have become such significant leaders in that world, that the IRS could not ever change that. They could make it more difficult, but it wouldn't change anything. People would dig deeper," George said in his office at the nonprofit Regas Institute in downtown Pasadena. "The whole business of the freedom of the pulpit is so central—not only for the progressive pulpit, but also for the conservative pulpit. The freedom to speak truth as you have come to understand it is very important. Anything that mitigates that is a huge impoverishment to being true to the message, true to what God's calling us to be."

All Saints believes it stands in the line of a prophetic tradition, "particularly of Isaiah, Hosea, Amos, and Jesus," Ed said. "Isaiah and Amos are very clear that God finds beautiful worship repugnant if it doesn't lead you to go into the world and change the world for the widows and the orphans and everybody who is disenfranchised and marginalized. All Saints is not about just showing up. All Saints is about showing up for beautiful, transformative, moving corporate worship, but it is always, always in the interest of taking the transformation you have experienced in worship to the world, to transform the world, so that it can be what God's dream always was when God created the world.

"The essence of my stewardship theology is the belief that we are God's colleagues. In order for us to be energetic, inspired, empowered colleagues of God, we have to put our money where our mouth is. When you give, you release so much more energy for God, because it's so energizing and inspiring to be a giver."

"The essence of my stewardship theology is the belief that we are God's colleagues. In order for us to be energetic, inspired, empowered colleagues of God, we have to put our money where our mouth is."

TWO INFLUENTIAL RECTORS

All Saints Episcopal Church celebrated its 125th anniversary in 2008, and the celebration included a $45 million capital campaign to expand space for worship, Christian education, and community activism. All Saints sits on prime real estate in Pasadena. City Hall is just across Euclid Street, and Fuller Theological Seminary is one block east. With its gothic architecture and well-tended courtyard, All

Saints is a picturesque campus that sometimes appears in films and television shows.

It would be tempting to think that All Saints is rolling in money. When people mention their assumptions about All Saints, "I tell them that we don't have deep pockets. We don't have an endowment of much more than $1 million, which is really just unheard of," Ed said. "We're not a member of the Consortium of Endowed Episcopal Parishes, and our $5 million budget comes from the giving of the people. We have a very small endowment, we get 5 percent from that, and we've got some revenue that comes in from our parking lot, but that's it. All the other stuff comes from pledges, some special gifts that we go out and get from time to time, and the offering plate. We have a lot of people who have modest incomes. In this economic downturn, we've had three people who suddenly were homeless because they lost their jobs." Parishioner Peggy Phelps, who has given the church $50,000 annually for the past decade, agrees that the endowment is comparatively small, and she bemoans it: "We have a smaller endowment here than the SPCA does. That's shocking."

All Saints has a long tradition of political engagement, but its emphasis on tithing appears more directly tied to the arrival of George Regas as its rector in 1967, and Ed Bacon's continuing emphasis on tithing since becoming rector in 1995. Both men say they had come to appreciate tithing before they arrived at All Saints. George learned of tithing's importance while serving as a vicar, fresh out of seminary, at a tiny mission in Pulaski, Tennessee. Two parishioners told him that if the mission hoped to ever have any money, he needed to talk about tithing. "My systematic entry into the tithing world was one of self-interest," he said.

A native of Tennessee, he had studied at the famously progressive Episcopal Theological School (now Episcopal Divinity School) in Cambridge, Massachusetts, and returned to his home state during the early stirrings of the civil-rights movement to lead a mission in what was then Ku Klux Klan country. "It was a hard three years, but they were an important three years and they were three years of growth."

From Tennessee he became rector of Grace Church in Nyack, New York, which had seven hundred communicants. After George served there for two years, his bishop, Horace Donnegan, appointed him chairman of the diocesan stewardship committee. George sought advice from one of his parishioners, Wheeler Conkling, who stressed that leaders teach tithing most effectively by relying on public testimonies given by tithers. "He was the most affluent person in Nyack who was in the heart of my ministry," George said. "He was a successful businessperson who was deeply committed to the ministry of the church and to tithing. When I could get Wheeler Conkling in Nyack to witness to his Christian discipleship and to what tithing had meant to him, you'd better believe people listened. Not only was he a successful businessperson, but he was the very heart of the ministry of the church."

"It was just a given in [my father's] life that he wanted to give back because this country had given him so much. Generosity meant that he gave back. That planted itself deeply in me."

George also credits his father for teaching him about generosity. His father came to the United States as a penniless immigrant from Greece and eventually became a moderately successful restaurateur. Because his father started his life in America in such need, "He was a very generous human being, and so generosity was just part of my growing up. He didn't know anything about tithing." His father often said that your checkbook tells the story of your priorities. "That was real for him. When we were talking about what we could do or not do, he would say, 'Look at the checkbook, son. Look where we're spending the money.' I can remember, as a young boy, being surprised at the amount of money he gave to Saint James Episcopal Church. I never asked him about it. I was too young. He died when I was twenty-one. I never talked to him about what motivated that. It was just a given in his life that he wanted to give back because this country had given him so much. Generosity meant that he gave back. That planted itself deeply in me."

Ed also credits his father, and the first priest he worked for in Atlanta, with teaching him about tithing. "My father was a Baptist minister and also an educator. He and mother always tithed. He preached tithing," he said. "When I began my career or vocation as an Episcopal priest, my boss, Dan Matthews, said, 'It's time for you to be tithing, and I know you know the importance of tithing. And you and Hope are not tithing. I want you to know that if you want to be a fruitful priest in the Episcopal Church, and you're going to be a rector of a church, it's important that you tithe, because of all the benefits.' I didn't have to ask him, 'What are the benefits?' I didn't resist that at all. I just said, 'You're absolutely right,' and so we immediately began tithing, and have ever since."

> *"If you want to be a fruitful priest in the Episcopal Church, and you're going to be a rector of a church, it's important that you tithe, because of all the benefits."*

WHY PEOPLE GIVE

Some of Ed's parishioners smile as they describe his challenging parishioners to give and then adds, "I hope I'm not asking too little of you." All Saints conveys its emphasis on tithing primarily through people giving their testimonies—speaking during church about how they have grown into more generous givers—and in related articles through the parish newsletter, *Saints Alive*.

"I think people intrinsically know that when they give, that's when they're happy, that's when they're joyful," Ed said. "I think that underneath that is something that they might never say: when you give of yourself, to a faith community and to others, that's one of the places where you get to discover the image of God that is within you. The essence of God is always to be giving. God is a giver. God is a giver of life; God is a giver of health; God is a giver of forgiveness; God is a giver of mercy and compassion; God is a giver of energy to transform the world to be a just and peaceful place. I think that there is a spiritual phenomenon that goes on when you give generously. The by-product is joy and happiness, but the deepest thing that is going on is that you're expressing the image of God within you. I think that people feel connected with God in a way that's as powerful as having a mystical experience during prayer or while gazing at the sunset."

Several members of All Saints reinforced Ed's perspective as they discussed their giving to the church. Vestry member Gloria Pitzer said that she and her husband were already increasing their giving when their life together took a challenging turn. "My husband lost his job, and all of a sudden we were tithing. I like to call it the case of the inadvertent tither," she said. "Living generously is learned. It's learned from hearing how other people are freed by doing it. I don't think you're born as a giver. It's freed me from the guilt of holding on to my money and worrying about what I'm going to part with. It's freed me to be generous in other giving as well."

> *"Living generously is learned. It's learned from hearing how other people are freed by doing it."*

Cooper Thornton moved to Los Angeles from Nashville to pursue acting. Cooper and his wife, Laura, an ordained minister, felt at home in the atmosphere of All Saints. "It's exciting for something so uncomfortable to be out on the table. You've named the elephant in the room," Cooper said of the church's emphasis on tithing. Cooper appreciates tithing as one of the several spiritual disciplines—such as prayer and serving the needy—that sometimes are easier to see in a liturgical church. "The disciplines just give much more of a shape to my life. It gives me a connection to a global faith community that shares a lot of the same disciplines."

Kate Gasparrelli-Byrne credits her parents' emphasis on generosity with helping her be open to tithing. "I don't like the word *tithing*. It sounds like a tax we pay to God," she said. Nevertheless, she tithes and considers generosity a crucial aspect of living as a Christian. "You can't make life like this," she said, clinching a fist. "You have to make life like this," she said, opening her hand again. "You can stretch and give at a level that's uncomfortable for you and trust that the universe will be there to support you. This is the heart of tithing: we are in this together. Tithing becomes a natural extension of how you aggregate what you care about. If you're not tithing, you're preventing the Holy Spirit from working in your life in a major way."

"This is the heart of tithing: we are in this together. Tithing becomes a natural extension of how you aggregate what you care about. If you're not tithing, you're preventing the Holy Spirit from working in your life in a major way."

Dottie Simmons, director of strategic planning and operations for Home Box Office, grew up in the African Methodist Episcopal Church. "I eventually got to a place where giving to God *first* meant I truly believed that my needs will be met regardless of my apparent circumstances in this material world," she said. "When I first began tithing, I made significantly less than I do now, so of course that 10 percent had more of an impact on my finances, but my thinking really changed. Within months I had enough money for all of my *needs* and I found myself *wanting* less."

Richard Beatty, who works at Jet Propulsion Laboratories, has taken his engineering skills on short-term visits to Armenia and Malawi through an All Saints program called Transformation Journeys. "I've never heard it as required or that you're a bad person if you don't tithe," he said. "Rather, it's been an invitation. It makes me feel a lot more of a bond with the place, more informed, and much happier to be a part of it."

When many of these All Saints parishioners discussed their lives of giving, they also mentioned Warrington "Warry" MacElroy, a longtime member of All Saints. "Have you talked to Warry?" they said. "You have to talk to Warry."

Warry, who is retired, made himself available on short notice during my final day of meeting with members of All Saints. He was dressed in casual but elegant clothes, but the more striking thing about him was a ready smile and eyes that radiated peace. "Up until 1973, I was a respectable Christian, I was a good boy. I did what I was supposed to do," he said.

Then he attended Cursillo[1] and became a born-again and charismatic Christian. Through a friend at work, he saw a pro-tithing pamphlet published by Seventh-day Adventists. He read the pamphlet, was impressed by its message, and felt that God said to him, "Warry, after all

I've done for you, do you think I would ask you to tithe and not make it possible for you to do that?"

He had to triple his donations to reach 10 percent. "Now I'm scared to stop," he said. "I have no desire to stop. It's what we're supposed to be doing. It is one of the most simple and direct ways of discovering an up close and personal God." Like Stacy Kramer of New Orleans, Warry cites God's words in Malachi 3:10: "'Test me in this,' says the LORD Almighty, 'and see if I will not throw open the floodgates of heaven and pour out so much blessing that you will not have room enough for it.'"

LIVING WATER

When Ed Bacon talks with new members of All Saints—or with members who otherwise need help in learning some principles of generosity—he compares the two very different bodies of water that he saw during a tour of Israel. First, he describes the vibrancy surrounding the Sea of Galilee, which he witnessed from the deck of a restaurant at the seashore. "There were people in rowboats and speedboats, folks way out in fishing boats, people on Jet skis, people picnicking along the banks. For centuries people have made their business a fishing business because the place is so full of fish," he said.

"Next, I talk about going to the Dead Sea on the same tour, and there's no life there. The only thing that's going on is in one or two spots you go and get this mud on your face and it's supposed to be good for your skin. You can go out and float because of all the salt. But there is no boating, no picnicking, no foliage, no greenery. It's desolate.

"That is the essence of life, and that is the essence of what makes you alive, when you not only receive the graces of God but you also give the graces of God away very liberally, very generously."

"The difference between those two bodies of water is that the Sea of Galilee not only receives the Jordan River, but it releases the Jordan River; it gives. The Dead Sea only has water coming in. Nothing is flowing out, except through evaporation. That is the essence of life, and that is the essence of what makes you alive, when you not only receive the graces of God but you also give the graces of God away very liberally, very generously."

10

"DO THEY TELL SUCH STORIES ABOUT ME AND YOU?"

Yisroel Miller

ABOUT TWENTY-FIVE THOUSAND JEWS LIVE IN GREATER Pittsburgh, and the largest concentration of Jewish families is in the neighborhood known as Squirrel Hill. Visit Squirrel Hill on a Friday evening or a Saturday, and you will see steady streams of people walking, sometimes in the middle of side streets, to the neighborhood's eight prominent synagogues, including Congregation Poale Zedeck, at the corner of Shady and Phillips avenues. This Orthodox synagogue, where Austro-Hungarian immigrants worshipped beginning in the late nineteenth century, is rich in stained glass. The Pittsburgh History and Landmarks Foundation helps support and protect this gem of a sacred space.

I arrived early for an afternoon interview with Yisroel Miller, who became the rabbi of Poale Zedeck in 1984.[1]

I walked around the block and then sat on the front steps of the building, enjoying the whimsical manner in which Shady Avenue branches off and forms a triangular corner with Tillbury Avenue. A man opened the door from behind me. "Are you the rabbi?" I asked. He was instead the building's caretaker, he told me good-naturedly. After I explained I was there to interview Rabbi Miller, he wished me a pleasant visit to "Congregation PZ," as he called it.

The office entrance for Congregation PZ is protected by an intercom system, but I arrived at the door at an opportune moment and walked in behind an older member of the congregation. A staff member seemed nervous about my unexplained presence until I mentioned that I was there to see Rabbi Miller.

The rabbi greeted me warmly, and we stepped into a study lined with hundreds of books, most of them in Hebrew. As an air conditioner hummed in one corner, we sat, and the rabbi was soon walking me through Orthodox Jewish thinking on tithing in a patient voice of instruction. Our conversation was not strictly catechetical, but Rabbi Miller is a man who loves to teach—not merely because it is his role in this congregation, but also because he loves and reveres the law that he's explaining.

"My father was a rabbi. Growing up in a rabbinic home, the one thing that was clear to me was that I did not want to become a rabbi," he said. "I'm sure that's true of many clergy children. But I had an interest in the study of Jewish learning, which we call Torah. In Judaism, the study of your religion is a sacrament, one of the outstanding religious deeds one does, and as a teenager I met some charismatic people who gave me an insight into the fire of Jewish learning. I spent several years doing that, and I found I wanted to share it with other people.

"I eventually came to Pittsburgh on a fellowship program, after ordination, which allowed me to continue some of my studies and reach out to laypeople who wanted to study and learn more about Judaism, both those who are already committed and those who are searching. One of the places I did my teaching was in this synagogue. When the rabbi moved on, the congregation turned to me and asked, 'Would you be our spiritual leader?' That had not been my career plan, but I had a mentor—it's very important in our tradition to have a living mentor—and he said, 'If they ask you, you don't say no.' I took the position, and now I've been here twenty-four years."

INTERPRETING TORAH

On that warm summer day, Rabbi Miller's instruction was methodical. He defined the law that God gave through Moses, he explained today's prevailing consensus interpretations of that law, and he provided examples of righteous Jews who have lived in accord with the law.

"Among the commandments in the five books of Moses is that of tithing. Tithing is from agricultural produce, and the staples in ancient Israel were grain [wheat and barley], wine, and olive oil," he said. "Our tradition is that Jewish farmers in the land of Israel are to tithe those, which are given to those in need. When we change from an agricultural society to an urban one, and money becomes the medium of exchange, the question is, is there an obligation to take tithes from other forms of income? The consensus opinion is that there is an obligation.

"The general consensus is that giving tithes is a commandment, a fulfillment of God's will."

"But it's a question again: is that the original obligation of the Bible, or is it something the rabbis added? If it's something the rabbis added, it's still seen as something God wanted to be in agricultural society. Since now we are making money other ways, God would certainly want the idea of charity to continue. There are those of the opinion that, although tithing is a commandment, you find in Judaism a distinction between an obligation that has virtually no exceptions or a righteous deed that may not be a binding obligation. The general consensus is that giving tithes is a commandment, a fulfillment of God's will. To give a tithe to a charity is an obligation. To give a tithe of one's income may be very difficult for some people, and it's generally not seen as a binding obligation that everyone must do. It is something to be encouraged, though.

"We are a religion of law, and I should explain that. Many people think that once you put things into law codes, you drain the life out of them. There's always that danger, but we feel that as long as it's amorphous, it's not coded that this is what you need to do, human beings will stretch any obligation infinitely. By codifying it into law, we say, 'This is what you do.' We're not trying to take the spirit out of it.

"We have books on virtually every commandment to fulfill. 'Honor thy father and mother.' All right—Jews, Christians, people around the world, are in favor of that, but Jews have books on the subject. What does that mean? 'Do not go about as a tale-bearer.' Most people consider that proper conduct. We consider it a biblical commandment. As such, there are laws on it, and people study books of law on what it means to gossip. What may one say, what may one not say, when may one make exceptions? The effect of the study is not to take the spirit out of the law. On the contrary, it sensitizes you to it. On a day when I'm studying the laws about 'thou shalt not gossip'—which of course are always the writer's exhortations, essentially, and stories—when I'm studying one of those books, on that day I tend to gossip less than I would otherwise. It makes me a more spiritual being. The same thing is true with the laws of charity in general and tithing in particular."

The third chapter of Malachi is a central focus of rabbis' teachings on tithing. Rabbi Miller said, "The rabbis say, based on a verse in one of the prophets where God says, 'Test me in this. Bring the tithe to the storehouse and see if I do not give you blessings without end.'[2] The Talmud says on this that in general it's wrong to test God. You can't say, 'Well, God, I'm going to pray really hard today, and I better win the lottery tonight or else. That's the test if you're really here.' As Woody Allen said, 'Send me a sign, like a deposit in a Swiss bank.' The Talmud says do not test God. Don't expect a payoff. An exception when you may test God: start giving a tithe, and see if you don't get paid back. I'm not sure there's a guarantee, or perhaps the payment will be in other forms, besides monetary. But in general, devout Jews like to say, nothing bad will happen if you're giving charity. Don't worry about becoming impoverished, but we're not talking about giving away all your income. But giving a tithe—our tradition is, it's good for you."

> "An exception when you may test God: start giving a tithe, and see if you don't get paid back . . . In general, devout Jews like to say, nothing bad will happen if you're giving charity."

LEARNING GENEROSITY BY STORIES

Rabbi Miller tells the story of how one act of non-ostentatious kindness created a cross-generational blessing between two families. "There was a rabbi, and someone in a neighboring community passed away, leaving behind a widow and an orphaned child. They were destitute. This was a couple of generations ago. The rabbi helped raise money for the widow and the orphan. The orphan went on to become the dean of a major rabbinical school. Of course, the orphan knew nothing about the rabbi who had helped his family when he was a child. The rabbi's grandson wanted to become a rabbi, and he went to a certain school and didn't do well. He was a round peg in a square hole. So he tried another school. It was like a prep school. When you're going for the rabbinate, there are prep schools. He went to a couple of schools and was unsuccessful.

"So someone said to him, 'Why don't you go visit the dean of this very prestigious rabbinical school? It's like a grad school. He's a very wise man.' So this kid went to the dean, the rabbi, and the dean said, 'Why don't you enroll here?'"

The student was doubtful that he could do any better at this prestigious school, but the dean persuaded him to audit classes and to live with the dean as he made the transition back into academic studies.

"So the young man ended up living in the rabbi's house. The dean got him into the school against five thousand normal regulations. The young man ended up in the school. Today's he a very successful rabbi in New Jersey," Rabbi Miller said. "I know the young man, and I know the great rabbi, the dean. And if you'll tell me it's a coincidence that the young man's grandfather helped the orphan, who does not know this, and that this dean of students felt the need to help this young man, I just see it as one simple example of payback. There are many such stories."

Rabbi Miller cites two works in English, written primarily for contemporary Jews who do not know Hebrew or whose knowledge of the language is very limited. One book is *Guide to Halachos* [laws]: *A Quick Reference Manual of What You Can Do in Common Occurring Situations.*[3] Another provides an English translation of teachings on tithing by Rabbi Israel Meir Kagan (1840–1883), who began writing anonymously as a Polish grocer but eventually achieved a sustained influence on Orthodox Jews across the world.[4] Both books provide clear explanations of how to calculate what one should give in a year, and describe options on how to distribute that money. The emphasis is more on charitably meeting other people's needs than on supporting the synagogue as an institution.

Rabbi Kagan is better known as Chafetz Chaim, after his first book, and many stories tell of his godly life. "His wife wanted him to study," Rabbi Miller said. "She ran the store most of the day, and he studied, and when he was forty years old, he saw that there were many Jews who are not aware that gossip is sinful. It's not a nice thing to do, but you wouldn't think of it like someone who embezzles from the bank. He said, 'Thou shalt not steal. It's a sin. Thou shalt not bear tales. It's a sin.' There are books about honesty in business. There were no books written about tale-bearing. It's mentioned, but a whole book? He wrote a whole book on the subject, followed by another book. He published it anonymously. He wasn't looking for honor. The book is called *Who Wants to Live?* or *Who Wants Life?* In Hebrew, it's *Chafetz Chaim*.[5] Since people did not know his name, it was anonymous, they referred to the author of this book as Chafetz Chaim, and that's the way he's known till this day. He went on to write many other books, including a book on general obligations toward others, in which he includes the obligation, the commandment, the mitzvah, of tithing."

Rabbi Miller continued: "They tell stories about him that I would not believe, except that I have met his students. He had a student from Germany. Russia was fighting Germany, and he was arrested as a spy. So Chafetz Chaim, Rabbi Kagan, was called to the stand as a character witness. The attorney wanted to explain to the judge, 'Who is this man?' So the attorney said, 'Your honor, I'll tell you a story about this man. He was one day walking on the street and someone stopped him and asked if he could change a ten-dollar bill. So Chafetz Chaim pulled out his wallet and started to make the change, and that person grabbed the wallet and started running down the street. Chafetz Chaim, an elderly man already, started running after him, saying, "I forgive you! I forgive you!"' So the judge said to the attorney, 'You believe that story is true?' The attorney said, 'I don't know, Your Honor, but do they tell such stories about me and you?'"

One reason for Chafetz Chaim's widespread respect, Rabbi Miller believes, was that he *lived* the tradition. "If you talk about the outstanding rabbis, to be on the very top rung of those who are respected, you need a combination of outstanding scholarship and outstanding character. If you are a professor of Talmudic studies and you know a lot but the character doesn't seem to match, even if you're a decent fellow, you'll never make the top rung—partly because it's not an official position. It's accepted, and people tend to accept those they feel are living the tradition. The person who follows the rituals but does not have love for his neighbor is not following the tradition."

Modern secular culture is making it more difficult for people to appreciate generous giving as an individual and personal action.

Rabbi Miller is concerned that modern secular culture is making it more difficult for people to appreciate generous giving as an individual and personal action. He mentions going on a tour to Israel in a group of one hundred and fifty people, and giving each person one dollar to share with a needy person. Some members of the tour were so stumped by that simple opportunity that they asked if they could give their money back to the rabbi and let him distribute the money.

"It's hard to give away your money, but if as soon as you get your paycheck you put 10 percent into your charity checking account, then it's not yours anymore," Rabbi Miller said. In the Jewish tradition, "You're not allowed to give all your tithe in one place. You have to be available if people need you for something. If a poor person, someone in need, comes knocking at your door, you can't say, 'Well, I gave all my money to some other cause.' One has to reach out to a variety of causes. For instance, an Orthodox Jew will make sure to give a certain amount of charity to people in need and give another certain amount of charity to the meaning and maintenance of Judaism—the synagogue, schools. In our faith, study is so important, to support a Jewish school that teaches Judaism is vital. Generally, we tell people that if the community has a choice of one building, either a synagogue or a school for children, make it the school. If you have the school, you'll end up with a synagogue. If you have a synagogue and no school, you'll end up with neither.

In the Jewish tradition, "You're not allowed to give all your tithe in one place. You have to be available if people need you for something."

"There are many people who ask me if they're allowed to use their tithe in other ways." The rabbi mentions the giving of some members of his congregation. "I know there is someone who has a charity account. He said to me, 'Rabbi, if you ever know of anybody in need, let me know.' I'll tell him about a case now and then, usually without the name, and he'll send me a check. There are good people everywhere, and it is so inspiring to see people who are charitable and it gives them joy. Occasionally rabbis will come to town for various causes, like a major rabbinical school in Israel, or a major rabbinical school in New York City, and I'll write a letter of recommendation, give their contacts. There was a gentleman—he has passed on since—he was not a learned Jew, but he had done well in business, and he said to me, 'Rabbi, if you ever have anybody visiting who's collecting for something you think is worthy, please bring him around.' I would bring someone to him. It's not just that he would welcome people with a smile. Afterward he would call me and say, 'Thank you so much for bringing that person to me, that I could help him out.' There are a number of souls like that.

"There are others who use their tithing to give support to families in need without their knowing where the support comes from. Or even better, sometimes, do it in a way that they don't even know that they're getting a gift. For instance, to hire someone to do a service and to pay them extra—and they don't realize that the extra is a way of helping them."

Rabbi Miller said that one of his mentors emphasized the principle of tithing one's time and treasures just as much as tithing one's income. Such service takes a variety of forms. "There are Jewish funeral homes, but we have volunteers who do special bathing and clothing of the dead, and the honors to be done to them. People give of their time to do that. It's a tithe of one's time, to help prepare dead bodies for burial. There are people in New York City who started an ambulance service. Because of the nature of New York, if someone needs an ambulance, one can wait quite a while. Some orthodox Jews, a few decades ago, made a private ambulance service, and it's staffed totally by volunteers. You don't have to be Jewish to use it, and they don't put it in the Yellow Pages, because if everyone would use it, they would not have enough people to staff it. But it's there, and there are volunteers who go out, and virtually every large synagogue in New York has people who belong to that organization, who are trained to give CPR, first aid, whatever it takes.

> *"There are imaginative ways of giving of one's time, beyond giving of one's financial resources."*

"I know other people who volunteer, who give of their time. If you don't have AAA and your car breaks down, people are available twenty-four hours a day in shifts. There are imaginative ways of giving of one's time, beyond giving of one's financial resources."

11

RIGHTEOUS NUMBERS
CRUNCHING

John and Sylvia Ronsvalle

THE MINISTRY KNOWN AS EMPTY TOMB, INC., IS BASED
in a modestly sized office building within walking distance
of the University of Illinois at Urbana-Champaign. In
the weeks before I met with its founders, John and Sylvia
Ronsvalle, I suggested a discussion of about an hour. Sylvia
responded with a more generous and open-ended schedule
that included lunch followed by a lengthy interview. The
Ronsvalles met me at the Champaign train station, graciously helped me arrange for an earlier return to Chicago
that evening, and gave me a driving tour of the university
campus. As we drove past Memorial Stadium, the imposing brick structure where the Fighting Illini play football,
the Ronsvalles talked about how many people collectively
spend hundreds of thousands of dollars annually to secure
coveted skyboxes there.

Sylvia describes empty tomb, which the Ronsvalles founded in the early 1970s, as a Christian research and service organization. That's an understatement on the order of saying the Salvation Army occasionally helps a homeless person. Sylvia says, "When we chose the name in the early 1970s, the lower case was an attempt on our part to state, in a non-triumphalistic way, that Jesus did, indeed, rise from the dead, and to state that truth in a casual and accessible fashion." For reporters writing stories about the state of giving in churches, empty tomb is the go-to think tank. The Ronsvalles crunch statistics so vigorously that in 2010 they plan to publish the twentieth edition of *The State of Church Giving*, a challenging report of nearly two hundred pages.[1] They praise whatever progress they find, such as the decision of Cornerstone Church in Simi Valley, California, to devote half its budget to missions. Still, they also catalog just how little priority most churches give to worldwide evangelism or to fighting preventable childhood deaths in developing nations.

Recent subtitles of *The State of Church Giving* offer some hint of what the Ronsvalles think as they survey the landscape each year: "Abolition of the Institutional Enslavement of Overseas Missions" (2007), "Global Triage, MDG 4 [Millennium Development Goals], and Unreached People Groups" (2008). On the back cover of the 2008 edition, they add a trio of Bible verses, all of which include the numbers 3:16 and convey God's concern for transforming the world:

John 3:16: "For God so loved the world, that he gave his only begotten Son, that whosoever believeth in him should not perish, but have everlasting life." (KJV)

1 John 3:16–17: "This is how we know what love is: Jesus Christ laid down his life for us. And we ought to lay down our lives for our brothers. If anyone has material possessions and sees his brother in need but has no pity on him, how can the love of God be in him?" (NIV)

The Revelation to John 3:16: "So, because you are luke-warm, and neither cold nor hot, I am about to spit you out of my mouth." (NRSV) [2]

But empty tomb is not just a research organization. The *service* part of its mission statement includes helping the poor of Champaign with food, clothes, furniture, bills, home repair, prescription costs, layettes for newborns, and Christmas gifts. Much of empty tomb's building is devoted to storing supplies that local Christians donate and help distribute to the needy.

One interior wall, which bears the weight of the struc-ture, honors the members of many churches that donated money and labor during construction. Church members signed the two-by-fours behind the wall.

Sylvia recalls that when she and John began their work among the poor, some black children in Champaign had red hair because of malnutrition. "There was dire poverty, and many churches were not involved," she said. "We just started saying, 'Jesus cares,' and people in need would start showing up on our doorstep." The Ronsvalles began helping people in immediate need of clothing, food, or furniture. "The local work started because we saw need. We met people. They needed food. From there we started asking, 'What more can we do?'"

The Ronsvalles began with a larger vision than merely helping the poor on behalf of people who did not want to get involved with the poor. Sylvia quotes what John emphasized from the beginning of empty tomb: "We're not going to take care of the poor. We are going to provide discipleship opportunities." When a woman from one church began delivering food, she told other church members about her experiences. Another hundred people from that church signed up to join their sister in similar ministry. "It's important for people to meet people—and then, suddenly, you can love them," Sylvia said. "The bigger ideas make sense because they grow out of this care."

"SHE JUST WANTS TO SAVE THE WORLD"

Concern for the poor and for evangelizing the world weaves through the Ronsvalles' years together. Except for a year of teaching English in China, they've spent their married life together in this small university town. John and Sylvia had met on campus, but John really caught Sylvia's attention in December 1969, when they saw each other in a pub near the university campus. The pub meeting occurred just after Sylvia had accompanied her sister Mary to watch a documentary about Vietnam. "I was in a power struggle with God during my junior year in college on who would be in charge of my life," Sylvia said. "It all came to a head one night. My sister, who was into bands and traveling, came down, and we were going out to the bars. She, of all things, said, 'Let's go and watch some television.' There was a show on the Vietnam War.

"As I was watching, as they were talking to this general about how they were going to now put the Vietnamese in charge as the Americans pulled out, I saw big white letters across the TV screen that said *death*. It was clear to me, and it said everything apart from Jesus Christ leads to death. I was Miss Let's Make Everything Fine. I ran out of the viewing room in tears and ran into the bathroom. I decided that I had to quit school the next day and be a missionary, because that's one of the things I felt God wanted."

From there, Sylvia and Mary went to the pub. John, who was general chairman of the Graduate Student Association, walked in and sat at the table with Sylvia and Mary. He asked, "What's wrong with Sylvia?"

"Nothing. She just wants to save the world," Mary said.

"That was like red meat to John," Sylvia told me. "My sister left the table, he sat down, and he started this two-hour sentence about how you get students on the faculty senate at the University of Illinois and you eventually evangelize the world for Jesus Christ. It all connected, through many rivulets. As he was talking, just as I had heard that everything apart from Jesus Christ leads to death, the same Voice said, 'I want you to help this man. You've been so busy telling me what you wouldn't do, you couldn't hear what I wanted you *to do*. I want you to help this man.'"

Sylvia agreed to help John. "That's when I signed up, and he started taking me out for dinner. We were working on getting students on the faculty senate every night. And I thought, *Thank you, God; at least you've given me a rich man*. It turned out he was spending all his savings in a very irresponsible fashion," she said.

John laughed quietly.

"When we got married, we were poor-poor," Sylvia said. "I'm talking *food stamps* poor-poor. We lived in an unoccupied house and eventually moved into public housing." During their last six years in public housing, the Ronsvalles did not take a rent subsidy from the government, and they ended up paying more for their public housing than some friends paid on mortgages.

The Ronsvalles lived in a public housing project known as Bradley Park. "We moved in there, and it was pretty scary. We found water all over the floor, and it turned out that it was raw sewage that had backed up in these apartments since they were built," Sylvia said.

The Ronsvalles began a years-long campaign that involved bucking officials with the Department of Housing and Urban Development, who insisted that residents of the public-housing complex were causing the sewer problems. Eventually the Ronsvalles helped convince the city council to authorize a study of the sewer problem. The study proved that the sewer lines had been installed incorrectly, and the majority of apartments were repaired.

"We can't just live someplace. It has to make a difference in the kingdom," Sylvia said, laughing lightly.

MOVING AT SCALE

Listening to John Ronsvalle gives some idea of the intensity behind empty tomb's name for itself. "If Jesus Christ really, really got up from the dead, and was really, really God, that's pretty big news; that's very, very important," he said. "It's hard to convey now the sense I had in high school that, 'If this is true, wow!' Everything else falls by the wayside in terms of importance. But it didn't seem like people were taking it that seriously."

If Christians truly believe that Jesus Christ conquered

death with his physical resurrection, and that he will return to earth someday as both triumphant king and the righteous judge of humanity, they ought to behave accordingly, John reasons. They ought to make financial choices that give top priority to God and his purposes. The church, to use one of John's favorite themes during our interview, ought to "move at scale."

If Christians truly believe that Jesus Christ conquered death with his physical resurrection, and that he will return to earth someday as both triumphant king and the righteous judge of humanity, they ought to behave accordingly.

"We are not moving at scale. We are playing at Christianity," John said. To drive his point home, John relies on an observation from the Southern Baptist Convention that 2,800 missionaries could complete the job of reaching all remaining people groups that have never heard the gospel of Jesus. Assuming a cost of $65,000 for each missionary, the total cost of world evangelism would be $182 million.[3]

That sounds like a lot, but John tosses other numbers in for context: About 1.14 million American households have a net worth of $5 million or more. Using a very strict doctrinal definition of the word *evangelical*, roughly 7 percent (or nearly 80,000 households) of evangelicals have a net worth of $5 million or more, with an annual income of about $400,000. Now consider: Americans spend $70 billion per year on soft drinks. A mere $5 billion a year would stop child deaths from preventable diseases around the world.

Repeatedly during our interview, John returned to the figure of $182 million, and of how easy it would be to achieve: a mere 2 cents per day in evangelical churches. He refers to the failure to meet this need as outrageous and scandalous. "During the last thirty-five years that we've been active, two major things have happened. One, Franky Schaeffer called for getting arrested for protesting abortion. And, more recently, the Micah Challenge; they're really gearing up on the Millennium Development Goals."

John is frustrated that both those cases of social involvement primarily amount to asking that *governments* help relieve suffering. "In all of this, there's no mobilization to get this job done," he said, whacking his papers of statistics that show an achievable goal of world evangelism.

"I think it's poor political science to ask people to vote to do something they won't do voluntarily," Sylvia said. "What we saw in a lot of the major social movements was generally an overflow out of the church of personal convictions, and those people convinced people. Abolition, the women's movement, the prison reform movement, child labor laws—all of these grew out of actively concerned church people who were there out of faith, and then it became more efficient to do it governmentally."

"We hear about winning the world for Christ, and I

don't think we're very seriously working at that in any intelligent way," John said. "It seems like the Great Commandment is a major directive that Jesus gave us, and it seems like the Great Commission is easily seen as flowing from the Great Commandment. Why do we want to see somebody become saved? It's out of love for them. If we love them, word and deed come together."

> *"The Great Commission is easily seen as flowing from the Great Commandment. Why do we want to see somebody become saved? It's out of love for them. If we love them, word and deed come together."*

"OUR MONEY *IS* US"

The Ronsvalles decided early on that they would tithe. "I did not come from a tithing household, and as far as I know, John didn't," Sylvia said. "We had two rooms to live in and seventy-five dollars a month plus food stamps and empty tomb's vehicle and phone line. We would occasionally get a doughnut at Eisner's. I remember the exact moment we decided to tithe. We were in the parking lot; we were driving a '56 Ford pickup. We were in our jeans—I had two pairs of jeans and five tops—and I said to John, 'John, we don't tithe.' He looked at me and we both said, 'Yeah, but we're so poor.' We looked at each other, and we agreed we had to tithe. That was the end of the discussion."

The Ronsvalles tithe on their donation-based income and on the value of their medical coverage. They donate a lot back into empty tomb. John understands Matthew 23:23 as Jesus' implicit affirmation of the tithe as the starting point for a person concerned with righteousness ("Woe to you, teachers of the law and Pharisees, you hypocrites! You give a tenth of your spices—mint, dill and cumin. But you have neglected the more important matters of the law—justice, mercy and faithfulness. You should have practiced the latter, without neglecting the former").

They set aside 10 percent with each new pay period, usually distributing it to a church and causes as they see needs arise. "Actually it's kind of fun to have that money set aside," Sylvia said. "You have it, it's there, and you see the need. It's not like 'Oh, I wish I could help,' but 'How much do we want to give here?' It becomes, 'What does God want to do?'"

For the Ronsvalles, tithing is not only a matter of obeying God. It is also a conscious way to resist the self-worship that accompanies greed and stinginess.

For the Ronsvalles, tithing is not only a matter of obeying God. It is also a conscious way to resist the self-worship that accompanies greed and stinginess. "One of the things we've concluded is that our money *is* us," Sylvia said. "It's a direct function of who we are. It's two concepts. One is of our current time and talent—our work, our energy, our volunteering. But money is really our *stored* time and talent. It's what we have invested and built up. Our parents, when you have an inheritance, that's them.

"The fact is, our money is just another form of us. Ephesians 5:5 and Colossians 3:5 both point out that greed is idolatry. Idolatry is worship, essentially, of self rather than God, which is why we cannot have any other gods. All other gods, besides Jehovah Yahweh, really come back to us. If we are not coming to terms with our money, there is a part of ourselves that we are worshipping, reserving from God, keeping from God. That's why tithing is a spiritual discipline, in the sense that it's really one of the most basic ways of coming to terms with idolatry. If you don't have your money in order, then you don't have yourself, in a very real sense."

In one essay they've published online, the Ronsvalles quote a fellow Christian as asking them, "If I'm not trusting God with my money, am I really trusting him with my eternal salvation?" Sylvia adds: "If we see money as a way to pay the bills, then whether I tithe is a consumer decision: 'Can I afford to live in a bigger house? Can I afford to tithe? Can I afford to take a vacation?' But if, in fact, I understand that money is nothing more than my efforts in a different form, then what I do with it directly has to do with my heart. It reflects who I am, where I'm investing myself."

After so many years of studying the world's needs and the church's poor giving patterns, the Ronsvalles struggle to reconcile the two. John said they sometimes think of Christians in comparison to two figures from J.R.R. Tolkien's Lord of the Rings trilogy: the Ents (slow-moving trees) and Théoden, the king who spends much of the narrative in an enchanted stupor.

"It's greed-induced apathy. It's like people in this country are under the influence of drugs, and it is the drug of affluence," Sylvia said. She cites Jacques Ellul's observation, in *Money and Power*,[4] that Jesus speaks of Mammon as a personal being in Matthew 6, and she elaborates on it. "Mammon is competing for your soul with God. The church in the United States, with all the blessings we've had, has had two choices: You can take those resources and lay them at God's feet, or you can be consumed by them and become like Théoden, become like the Ents, become drugged. It would take visionary moral leadership to wake people up, and you're not seeing it."

Still, the Ronsvalles have not reached a point of despair, and they are amused at the thought of retirement. "How do you ever stop speaking the truth? This isn't a career. This, is like, what we're stuck with. You just have to do this, like breathing," Sylvia said. "It's an issue of faith. We don't get to sign up for results. We sign up to speak the truth."

Epilogue

STEWARDSHIP IS A THANKSGIVING TO GOD

Thomas McGread

IN MID-SEPTEMBER 2008, I FLEW TO WICHITA, KANSAS, to talk with Monsignor Thomas McGread, a pioneer of stewardship in Catholic circles. Because of his vision for stewardship, members of parishes in the Diocese of Wichita may send their children to diocesan schools without having to pay tuition. Monsignor Thomas spent thirty-one years of his vocation, until his retirement in 1997, as the pastor of St. Francis of Assisi Catholic Church in downtown Wichita. He later also worked as stewardship director for the diocese. He brought to the parish and the diocese an approach to stewardship that challenged its members to ask how much of their time and talents they were returning to God in thanksgiving for his grace.

"Christ died for us, and that's why we go to Mass: to thank him. Stewardship is really a thanksgiving to God," he said while sitting in his small apartment. "We have all kinds of time for entertainment and for sports, yet we have no time for God. And yet we expect to end up in heaven. We want to *prepare* for that life. We called it a way of life rather than just a program. You want to live this way, living with Christ."

> *"Christ died for us, and that's why we go to Mass: to thank him. Stewardship is really a thanksgiving to God."*

This way of life included round-the-clock Adoration of the Blessed Sacrament, which Monsignor Thomas credits with drawing people closer to the heart of Jesus and—by natural extension—toward showing more of God's generosity.

Monsignor Thomas, who came to the Diocese of Wichita in the 1960s as one of eight immigrant priests from Ireland, still speaks with a moderate Irish accent. He is the kind of gentle old priest who, closing in on eighty when I interviewed him, will call a longtime parishioner "Child" as she calls him with a prayer concern. The monsignor is a man of no long speeches. He answers questions with more than yes or no, but he limits himself to simple statements of fact.

Though he helped the U.S. Conference of Catholic Bishops prepare a pastoral letter, "Stewardship: A

Disciple's Response,"[1] he is concerned that bishops some-times hinder progress on stewardship.

"The biggest drawback is that some of the bishops are kind of scared of stewardship, like they don't quite under-stand it," he said. "A lot of them think it's about money. Even when the bishops wrote the pastoral, they were worried about calling it stewardship. They wanted to call it 'Disciple's Response.' But we convinced them that *stewardship* was a bib-lical word. Christ talked about being a good steward quite a lot, so let's explain what it means. There's a whole lot more than money in the whole thing. The main thing was time."

"Every Scripture passage, practically, has something about stewardship in it."

In about 1983, Monsignor Thomas began presenting workshops for Catholic Stewardship Consultants of Augusta, Georgia. His health struggles—he's had six heart bypass surgeries, and his legs have failed him—prevent him from giving live presentations any longer, and the consultancy relies on video recordings from the monsi-gnor's healthier years.

In presenting a theology of stewardship to his people, the monsignor said, he relied on no curriculum: "Just the Bible. There's enough in the Bible for that. Every Scripture passage, practically, has something about stewardship in it."

What I find especially striking about the monsignor is

that he said so little about the legacy of his work that surrounds us. When I called ahead to arrange our interview, I had the impression that he might live in a suburban condominium or house. Instead, he lives in an assisted-care facility that is adjacent to the diocese's Spiritual Life Center, a sprawling conference center. The same campus includes a home for retired priests.

All of these buildings were constructed during Monsignor Thomas's years as the diocese's stewardship director. He did not volunteer this information, but he acknowledged it when I asked. Just to the east of the Spiritual Life Center is Ascension Cemetery, developed at the same time. Here lie some of the Irish priests who came to America at the same time as the monsignor. Here he will rest as well.

Though he is not as infirm as Pope John Paul II was in his final years of life, the monsignor reminds me of that pontiff. This is how saints grow old and prepare to meet God. After we talked, I walked through Ascension Cemetery, where I marveled at a towering golden sculpture of the risen Christ, which stares out across the flat Kansas plains. I found a section devoted to children's graves, and one was decorated with a small knickknack bearing the image of SpongeBob SquarePants.

All this redemptive use of land is possible because one priest challenged his small and mostly poor congregation to begin spending more time with God. Suddenly I was crying.

NOTES

Introduction

1. Michael W. Holmes, ed. and trans., *The Apostolic Fathers in English*, 3rd. ed. (Grand Rapids: Baker, 2006), 163–64, 165, 170.

2. Philip Schaff, *Sulpitius Severus, Vincent of Lerins, John Cassian*, "How Those Who Live Under the Grace of the Gospel Ought to Go Beyond the Requirement of the Law." Accessed June 10, 2009, through the Christian Classics Ethereal Library: http://www.ccel.org/ccel/schaff/npnf211.iv.vi.v.v.html.

3. Philip Schaff, *Fathers of the Third and Fourth Centuries: Lactantius, Venantius, Asterius, Victorinus, Dionysius, Apostolic Teaching and Constitutions, Homily*, "Of First-Fruits and Tithes, and After What Manner the Bishop is Himself to Partake of Them, or to Distribute Them to Others."Accessed June 10, 2009, through the Christian Classics Ethereal Library: http://www.ccel.org/ccel/schaff/anf07.ix.iii.iv.html.

4. Randy Alcorn, *Money, Possessions and Eternity* (Carol Stream, IL: Tyndale, 2003), 185.

Chapter 1: Continuity in the Tradition

1. Ephraim Radner and George R. Sumner, *Reclaiming Faith: Essays on Orthodoxy in the Episcopal Church and the Baltimore Declaration* (Grand Rapids: Eerdmans, 1993).

2. Frederica Mathewes-Green, *Facing East: A Pilgrim's Journey into the Mysteries of Orthodoxy* (New York: HarperSanFrancisco, 1996).

3. See Malachi 3:10.

Chapter 2: So That Others May Simply Live

1. Ronald J. Sider, *Rich Christians in an Age of Hunger: Moving from Affluence to Generosity* (Downers Grove, IL: InterVarsity, 1977).

2. Ronald J. Sider and Richard K. Taylor, *Nuclear Holocaust and Christian Hope: A Book for Christian Peacemakers* (Downers Grove, IL: InterVarsity, 1983).

3. Ronald J. Sider, *The Graduated Tithe* (Downers Grove, IL: InterVarsity, 1978).

4. Ibid., 3.
5. Ron Sider, "The Ministry of Affluence: A Graduated Tithe," *HIS* 33, No. 3 (December 1972), 6–8.
6. Sider, *Rich Christians in an Age of Hunger*, 44.
7. Jerry Kramer announced in September 2009 that he was leaving Annunciation and preparing to return to missionary work in Tanzania.

Chapter 4: Earnest Money

1. Metanoia Peace Community, "Glossary of Terms," s.v. "Non-Violent Direct Action," available at http://www.metanoiaumc.org/glossary2.htm.
2. Ibid., "A Brief History," available at http://www.metanoiaumc.org/briefhistory.htm.
3. Ibid., "Membership Covenant," available at http://www.metanoiaumc.org/membercovenant.htm.
4. Like some other progressive Christians, when John refers to the kingdom of God, he tends to the drop the letter *g*, as he believes that *kin-dom* sounds less patriarchal.
5. Paul Kirk and Pat Schwiebert, *When Hello Means Goodbye* (Portland: Oregon Health & Science University/Perinatal Loss, 1985).

Chapter 5: Treasures in Heaven

1. Amy Corneliussen, "Abortion Foes Face Resolute Opponent," *Los Angeles Times*, January 25, 1998. Available at http://articles.latimes.com/1998/jan/25/local/me-11913.
2. Randy Alcorn, *Is Rescuing Right?* (Downers Grove, IL: InterVarsity, 1990).
3. Genesis 50:20 NASB.

Chapter 6: "Never Tell Me What You Won't Do"

1. Jerald January and Steve Wamberg, *A Messed-Up Ride or a Dressed-Up Walk: A Stirring Autobiography of Hope for the City, Love for God, and a Faith That Stays the Course* (Grand Rapids: Zondervan, 1994).
2. Ibid., 12–13.

3. Jerald January, *A Second Time* (Hazel Crest, IL: CoolSprings Publishing, 1996).

4. John 14:2 KJV.

Chapter 7: Deep Gladness Meets Deep Hunger

1. Kevin Jones, "The Rise of the Right in the Republican Party," report from Indianapolis, November 2, 2002. Available at http://www.theocracywatch.org/Report_From_Indianapolis. html.

2. These and other articles are available at www.everyvoice.net/ archive.

3. Every Voice Network: Anglican Voices United for Justice, "About Our Team," Kevin Jones. Available at http://www. everyvoice.net/archive/modules.php?op=modload&name=Stat ic&mod=About2&file=index.

4. Good Capital, "FAQs," available at http://www.goodcap.net/ faqs.php.

5. Edmund Sanders and Robyn Dixon, "Dark Cloud over Good Works of Gates Foundation," *Los Angeles Times*, January 7, 2007. Available at http://www.latimes.com/news/la-na-gatesx07jan07,0,290910,full.story.

6. Frederick Buechner, *Wishful Thinking: A Seeker's ABC* (New York: Harper One, 1993, rev. ed.), s.v. "vocation."

Chapter 8: A Sense of Community

1. Theologians have written at length about the problems of the Worldwide Church of God's theology during its first sixty years of existence. By the mid-1990s, leaders of the church rethought the theology of founder Herbert W. Armstrong and ultimately repudiated it. In April 2009, the church changed its name to Grace Communion International.

2. Seventh-day Adventist Church, "Guidelines on the Use of Tithe," available at http://www.adventist.org/beliefs/ guidelines/main_guide4.html.

3. Ibid.

4. 1 Corinthians 10:26 KJV.

5. See 1 Corinthians 16:2.
6. See Hebrews 10:25

Chapter 9: "The Essence of God Is Always to Be Giving"

1. For more information on the Cursillo movement, see http://www.natl-cursillo.org/whatis.html.

Chapter 10: "Do They Tell Such Stories About Me and You?"

1. Yisroel Miller has since become the rabbi of the House of Jacob Congregation in Calgary, Alberta, Canada.
2. See Malachi 3:10.
3. Nachman Schachter and Moshe Heinemann, *Guide to Halachos: A Quick Reference Manual of What You Can Do in Common Occurring Situations* (New York: Feldheim, 2003).
4. *Ahavath Chesed: The Love of Kindness as Required by God* (New York: Feldheim, 1976).
5. *Chafetz Chaim: A Lesson a Day* (New York: Artscroll/Mesorah, 1995).

Chapter 11: Righteous Numbers Crunching

1. *The State of Church Giving Through 2006: Global Triage, MDG 4, and Unreached People Groups*, 18th ed. (Champaign, IL: Empty Tomb, Inc., 2008). Available at http://www.emptytomb.org/pubs.html.
2. Ibid., back cover.
3. Ibid., 65–67, 118.
4. Jacques Ellul, *Money and Power*, 2nd ed. (Downers Grove, IL: InterVarsity, 1985).

Epilogue: Stewardship Is Thanksgiving to God

1. "Stewardship: A Disciple's Response" (Washington, D.C.: United States Conference of Catholic Bishops, 2002), available at http://www.usccb.org/stewardship/disciplesresponse.pdf.